Along Came the Witch

Books by Helen Bevington

Helen Bevington

ALONG CAME THE WITCH

A
Journal
in the
1960's

Harcourt Brace Jovanovich
New York and London

Printed in the United States of America

Some of Helen Bevington's poems in this volume were first printed elsewhere: "The Asses of Alfoxden" appeared originally in her *Doctor Johnson's Waterfall* (Houghton Mifflin, 1946); "Barometers," in *The New Yorker;* "Categories," in her *When Found, Make a Verse Of* (Simon and Schuster, 1961); "Cry Nowel" and "The Happy Reader," in *The New York Times Book Review;* "Encounter with Crows" (as "November Noon"), "The Honeybee," and "A Royal Fable" (as "A Summer Fable"), in *The New York Times;* "A Launching for Ann," in *Southern Poetry Review;* and "Poet of the Grape" (as "The Poet Anacreon"), in the author's *A Change of Sky* (Houghton Mifflin, 1956).

The poem by Colin Falck, "The Tick," appears in his *Backwards into the Smoke,* copyright © 1973 by Colin Falck, published by Carcanet Press Limited, Manchester, England; the lines by Langston Hughes are from his "Dream Deferred," copyright 1951 by Langston Hughes, reprinted from *The Panther and the Lash: Poems of Our Times* by Langston Hughes, by permission of Alfred A. Knopf, Inc.; the poem "Sure," by Hugo Williams, is reprinted by permission of the author.

Library of Congress Cataloging in Publication Data

Bevington, Helen Smith, 1906–
    Along came the witch.

    Autobiographical.
    1. Bevington, Helen Smith, 1906–   —Biography
I. Title.
PS3503.E924Z495   811'.5'4 [B]   75-31653
ISBN 0-15-105080-5

First edition

B C D E

For Kate and the others, who are
not afraid of witches

Lost in the night, my love,
Are those who could never tell
The perishable world from the imperishable.

So they lived everafter, rich
In fairytales and in general—
Till along came the witch.

Along Came the Witch

1960

JANUARY. Who is brash enough to begin the new decade? Not I. Bertrand Russell is, at 88. He told his biographer, Alan Wood: "The secret of happiness is to face the fact that the world is horrible, horrible, *horrible*—you must feel it right here [hitting his breast] and then you can start being happy again."

So beating my breast, 1960, here I come.

Happy Coleridge: "For one mercy I owe thanks beyond all utterance—that, with all my gastric and bowel distempers, my head hath ever been like the head of a mountain in blue air and sunshine." His head rose up Vesuvian, rumbling and belching a little.

Colette: "Happiness? Come, what should I do with it?"

Horace: "Why is it, Maecenas, that no one is ever quite happy with the life he has chosen or stumbled upon, but loves to praise those who do something else? . . . So it is that you rarely find a man who admits to having been happy with the time allotted him and is ready to depart like a satisfied guest."
—*Satires*, I,1.

Hazlitt, on his deathbed: "Well I have had a happy life," and died alone in a bleak lodging in Soho, unloved, estranged after quarrels, "the dupe of friendship, and the fool of love." His first wife, Sarah Stoddart, divorced him. The woman he loved, Sarah Walker, refused him. The widow he married, Mrs. Bridgewater, left him. His essay "On the Pleasures of Hating" shows a vindictive man suffering from indigestion and bad temper. "Most of my friends have turned out the bitterest enemies or cold acquaintances." He kept his grudges and rage. "Have I not reason to hate and to despise myself?" He died happy.

3

Who can define the happy life? Not I.

As I drove to the University today, I met a car approaching at great speed, twisting through traffic. The driver swerved without quite killing either of us, but the sight of his anguished face unnerved me. It resembled my own. Then I recognized him: Duke University's happy man, Professor Hornell Hart, sociologist, authority on pure measurable happiness. He writes books about bliss, how to live serene, find peace, possess joy. One book is called *Autoconditioning*. And here he was in his auto, absenting himself from felicity awhile.

Happy is the way the fairytale ends, since happiness of course is what we mortals are entitled to. Why then is the crack of doom so often within hearing, a distant thundercrack not yet a sonic boom deafening to the ears but like a premonitory rumble of the planet breaking up?

I hear it in a toppling world, as everyone does. I heard it, for example, when I read Nabokov's *Lolita*, especially the rumble of the reviewers chuckling their way through this monstrous tale of the repeated rape of a little girl by a pervert and madman, finding the only word to describe it: "hilarious!" Even kindly old E. M. Forster was quoted at *his* age as saying, "It's a very funny book indeed, I thought." My lamentations are for him.

In times of hilarity like this, one can duck and cringe. Or one can turn again to a letter of Chekhov's for his comment on such depraved appetites: "It sometimes happens that one passes a third-class refreshment room and sees a cold fish cooked long before, and wonders carelessly who wants that unappetizing fish. And yet undoubtedly that fish is wanted, and will be eaten, and there are people who will think it nice. One may say the same of the works of N."

Jules Renard: "I am a happy man, for I have renounced happiness."

Now that we speak of fairytales, I admit I must have remembered them all wrong. What really happened was that, always before the enchanting story was done, along came the

witch. Here was the certainty you had to expect and face, the
one unfailing character to look out for who would make your
teeth rattle—along came the witch.

FEBRUARY. Nearly ten years ago I wrote a verse
about Dr. Johnson, who claimed he could get drunk on an
apple. It began,

> Dr. Johnson, drunk on an apple,
> With moral scruple
> Still would grapple.

Before the *New Yorker* printed it, they tried to check the
source of the quotation by telephoning Ned McAdam, professor of English at New York University. Ned replied he didn't
know, "but if Helen Bevington said Dr. Johnson said it, he
said it." I'm glad they didn't ask me.

Tonight while reading in bed, I laughed aloud when the
quotation turned up. It was bound to someday. Mrs. Thrale
told the tale in her notebooks, *Thraliana*, December 26, 1788,
four years after Johnson's death. She was a giddy woman, and
so am I.

People who keep journals may use them as a secret weapon.
Elizabeth (of the German Garden, the Countess Russell) found
after Katherine Mansfield's death how bored her cousin was
with her, how deep and bitter the resentment. Elizabeth herself left a journal of cruel revelations for her friends to wince
at. And Virginia Woolf—who knows how mortally she stabbed
others in the pages of her diary still unpublished while the
victims live? (She did call Katherine Mansfield callous and
hard, "content with superficial smartness.") Yet these women
never ruled out for a moment the likelihood of future publication. On page 3 of *A Writer's Diary*, Virginia Woolf speaks
of "my father Sir Leslie," hardly the way to talk to oneself of
a member of the family.

When a person writes for posterity, leaving words behind,
maybe he thinks of gazing down from a celestial region, out of

reach of any mortal wound. He will be safe. In the nothingness of death are no hurtful words.

Under "Diary" in the *Encyclopaedia Britannica:* "It is not necessary that the entries in a diary should be made each day, since every life, however full, must contain absolutely empty intervals." Edmund Gosse wrote that, whose *Father and Son* shows some absolutely empty intervals.

"Pleasant days make short journals," wrote Scott in his. Dull days make none at all.

On the other hand, Gilbert White of Selborne kept a daily journal for twenty-five years with some 10,000 entries. When he boiled up apricots with sugar to preserve them, or recorded "Wheeled dung," it was the notation of a living man. Two hundred years later it makes good reading. Dorothy Wordsworth, on Thursday, August 7, 1800, boiled up gooseberries and told in her journal how much sugar to add (2 lbs. to the panful). My own domestic entry is Great-aunt Lydia's recipe for dandelion wine:

Use equal quantities of boiling water and gold dandelion blossoms. Let stand 3 days and 3 nights. Strain, and to every gallon add 4 lbs. sugar, 4 lemons, I yeast cake. Allow to ferment to clear golden amber. Strain and bottle. Serve in tiny glasses to small children who will actually like it.

Further entry (value unknown): Chopped tiger whiskers make a good aphrodisiac.

My favorite journal is Jules Renard's. At night before sleep he counted over his images. In imitation of a wise thing I count mine, in alphabetical order, returning to the old familiar places—Afton, New York, where I was born and stayed only two weeks; Bath, Battersea Park, Brighton Pavilion. After several nights, with a pleasure trip to Cairo, I haven't got beyond middle C. There is Chicago where I visited my father Charley one summer after my parents' divorce. My father bends over me, and the game is ended. "Are you afraid?" he whispers to a sleepless child.

My image of him is like Jules Renard's of his "Papa. The

swollen veins of his temples. Moles are digging around and ravaging him under the skin." Charley's veins bulged like that when he ate, purpled when he was in a rage.

M A R C H .   At the Spring Break, a week's holiday from classes, B. took me to New Orleans to see a striptease. We didn't make the thousand-mile trip by car for that express purpose, yet on our return it's the first pleasure I recall, so perverse is memory. You never know which moment you will bring home.

In late March there were other fetching sights along the way: in Georgia, black Angus cows under the pecan trees ("Cows are my passion," said Mrs. Skewton in *Dombey and Son.*) In Alabama, miles of peach trees a calendar pink, after them the delicate beige flowering of the tung orchards. On the Mississippi Gulf Coast, a sweetfaced nun playing baseball on the beach with little boys.

All these fade beside the off-color activities on Bourbon Street. On Saturday night in the French Quarter, amid blasts of Dixieland jazz, we peered through doorways to catch sight of the naked girls, only to catch instead the eye of a pitchman who tried to cajole us inside for the peepshow.

B. said, "You choose. Which do you want to see?"

I hadn't realized I wanted to see any. Now it was decided, we made another tour of Bourbon Street, studying the girls' pictures and their vital statistics. Since I had the option, I picked Evangeline, the girl in the oyster shell. We had had oysters Rockefeller for dinner, which seemed to be the fruit of the locale.

Four girls performed that night in the smoky room with its long bar, twenty crowded tables, and tiny stage on which no drama more complicated than stripping had space to unfold. They were Evangeline, Sidney, Lola, and the last name I didn't catch. Each came on as a single.

Evangeline, the star stripper, rose at the finale in a misty garment like a pure white pearl out of an enormous bivalve. She might better have been billed as Dolores (Evangeline rings of Longfellow) and made a literary evening of it by reciting a little Swinburne:

Then love was the pearl of his oyster,
And Venus rose red out of wine.

One saw at once how expert she was. The illusion of pearly innocence, luster, sheen, radiance ("Through thy garments the grace of thee glows"), was dimmed somewhat by her bumps and grinds as she flung off wisps of white gauze in all directions—like a pearl out of its setting, like Dolores, fair daughter of Death and Priapus ("Come down and redeem us from virtue").

Still, it was an impressive lesson in how to escape from an oyster shell.

In the end I was taken with the girl Lola, who overcame still larger obstacles during her act to emerge winded but triumphant. Lola touched the heart. She was weighted down by clothes—scarves, petticoats, trinkets, gloves, plus a towering pineapple-laden headdress—so many separate items heaped upon her one groaned to think how long it would take to peel down to Lola. She was miscast as a performer. She couldn't writhe, shake, or twist her stout body in the proper teasing movements. It was a strain even by squinting or closing one eye to find her seductive, let alone carnal.

To make up for this lack of talent, Lola had prepared a pretty little surprise. With the flinging aside of the last pineapple, she smiled to warn us a great moment was at hand. The music stopped. She stood poised and bare in her G string as we held our breath, trembling with attention.

Out of the dark came a loud click. From somewhere on her person (I can't imagine where), Lola turned on an electric switch.

LOLA

Her name was Lola. And she did the striptease
On Bourbon Street, where you sit and watch the girls
While sipping Bourbon, or maybe the local absinthe,

Feeling not swindled but not hard to please
With all those girls—the girl in the oyster shell,
Cat girl, dove girl, girl with the peacock feather—
Identical and uniform in a G string,
Except for Lola. Lola in toto, well!
Lit up in lightbulbs there was a girl to see,
The way her breasts blinked on, off! on, off!
    on, off! gloriously.

In *Blue Skies, Brown Studies,* a book of travel, William
Sansom makes this nervous query: "Would one, socially, sit
naked with a blind woman?"

One might misquote Yeats: "There's more enterprise in
sitting naked." Or turn to Horace Walpole for the proper
etiquette for the unclad. During a trip to Paris, August 20,
1775, Walpole reported in a letter: "Madame du Deffand came
to me the instant I arrived, and sat by me whilst I stripped
and dressed myself; for as she said, since she cannot see,
there was no harm in my being stark." *Quelle délicatesse.*

Alexander Pope expressed a desire to see Lady Mary Wortley
Montagu's soul naked. "Without offence to your modesty be
it spoken, I have a burning desire to see your Soul stark naked,
for I am confident 'tis the prettiest kind of white Soul, in the
universe." This was before she laughed out loud and broke off
the romance.

Rabelais defined a naked person as one wearing "nothing
before, nothing behind, and sleeves of the same," which would
apply of course to both sexes.

The pride of the peacock is the glory of God.
The lust of the goat is the bounty of God.
The wrath of the lion is the wisdom of God.
The nakedness of woman is the work of God.
    —Blake, *Marriage of Heaven and Hell*

A P R I L .   I met Quentin Bell, son of our friends Vanessa
and Clive Bell, at the airport. What I didn't remember from
last seeing him in England is that he looks like Dante Gabriel
Rossetti.

He is red-bearded and commanding, very Pre-Raphaelite. He
bends at the waist. B. should produce him in his class in
Victorian literature and say, "Here before you, scholars, stands
an authentic late-Victorian." Actually, Quentin is timeless,
without convention or prejudice, any style of living (pre- or
post-Raphaelite) being agreeable to him.

We took him to a cocktail party, where he obediently drank
six martinis and remained calm. On his first visit to America,
he seemed unstartled by American heartiness. Though an
aesthete, he is dispassionate. Though he has written a book
about costume, *On Human Finery*, he is indifferent to dress,
his own or anybody's. He is a potter unaware of pots. He is a
modern painter (like his mother) and an art critic (like his
father) who ignores the pictures on the wall, out of politeness
and charity. Or out of a beautiful oblivion.

After three days, goodbye to Quentin, a gracious guest. I
told him in passing (God knows how I managed to bring it
up) that Bertrand Russell kissed me when he was eighty and
that I met the encounter in a daze of gratitude and delight. At
the airport Quentin turned in farewell and with touching
courtesy pecked me on the cheek. "That was for Bertie," he
said. I refrained from telling him in his gallantry how much
better at kissing Bertrand Russell was.

So, probably, was Dante Gabriel Rossetti.

M A Y .   Sir Herbert Read came and went at the tailend of
the year. He spoke last night at Duke on abstract art, explaining it as something murky dredged up from the unconscious.
The artist is apparently in luck to rid himself of it. Sir Herbert
showed no concern that art be pleasing. The idea of beauty or
ugliness or even meaning was never raised. Since he has said

modern poetry should be inaudible, I suppose modern art should be invisible. It seemed invisible to him.

I met him afterward at the Boyces'. Over the telephone Dorothy Boyce had cried, "They say he's a radical or something!" I said, "No, no, he's only an Anarchist."

In 1938 Herbert Read published *Poetry and Anarchism,* in 1940 *Philosophy of Anarchism.* But the Anarchists disowned him for supporting World War II, after he stoutly claimed "I do not accept war" and then accepted not only a world war but a knighthood in 1953. They swore he lied when he said he opposed the State and favored abolishing it.

In class I read my students his poem "Song for the Spanish Anarchists," and at the party (to make talk) told him so. He glowed. It was his finest poem, he said, which came to him all complete. I believe it. How else would this stanza come?

> And men are men who till the land
> and women are women who weave:
> Fifty men own the lemon grove
> and no man is a slave.

Sir Herbert is as mild and courtly an Anarchist as you would want to outface. Whitehaired and patrician in manner, he has a fragile charm—a softspoken man who doesn't look half as dangerous as he is. I mean dangerous to art and poetry.

On the whole, he seems to me a silly man. He thinks D. H. Lawrence a great poet and Lin Yutang a great philosopher. Max Beerbohm wrote a verse about him, "To Dr. D."

> Honoured Doctor Dryasdust,
> Look to your laurels: you really *must.*
> You seem so very moist indeed
> When one compares you with Herbert Read.

J U N E .   Commencement Day. It was an academic procession in the Duke Chapel with three Bevingtons in it, and there was tremendous applause when Philip received his doctor's

degree in his wheel chair. B. and I sat on the front row with
the faculty, and Joan his wife looked down from the balcony.
Philip's face was one of carved nobility. I thought, "The returns
are coming in."

Afterward, while people gathered around him, the friend
who was Phil's surgeon (following the automobile accident
that severed his spine) said to me, "He is in a class of heroes
by himself. He conquers on his own terms. A man of honor."

JULY.   Twelve white gardenia blossoms appear on the
Sears, Roebuck bush in the 100° heat. Let there be white
flowers for summer—white magnolias in the dooryard, white
petunias in the flowerbox, yarrow in the fields.

Four giant sequoias from California thrive on the porch in
tho hot sun. In their little pots, they are already trees one inch
high, starting from seed with 400 feet yet to grow tall and 40
feet round. An avocado plant with no claim whatever to im-
mortality towers over their prickly green heads. Give them
time. Give them another three or four thousand years.

For the past three summers I've gone with B. each weekday
to Duke University to sit in my office at a typewriter high in
an academic tower, where I was airconditioned, thriving,
happy. It was a safe retreat from students and thunderstorms,
and I had lunch each day with my colleagues, fortunately all
male.

This summer it cost B. two thousand dollars to keep me
home. By installing a system of ducts, pipes, and a purring
noise, he cooled me off, dusted his hands, then returned alone
to his office. Now I switch on the air conditioner, close the
doors, and go out on the porch to sweat at my typewriter.
There is the green meadow and the hum—a hummingbird in
the mimosa, the hum in my head of a word warming up.
Nobody comes near, not a Jehovah's Witness or an Avon lady.

When B. discovered I stay outside, 30° hotter than within,
he asked a loud plaintive why? "Sorry, love, I'm stifled in the

house." He laughed and quoted Pope, "Oh odious, odious trees!"

Papillia, wedded to her amorous spark,
Sighs for the shades—"How charming is a park!"
A park is purchased, but the Fair he sees
All bathed in tears—"Oh odious, odious trees!"

On July 17, 1689, which was 271 Julys ago, Madame de Sévigné wrote to her daughter: "The north wind doth blow and we shall have snow. And who cares?"

WHO CARES?

Squanderer, unthrift, choosing
Extravagance of days,
Wasting a fortune living,
Taking in wastrel ways
Time out to cuddle beggars,
A lavisher, a scandal
(As if you had forever
To burn the golden candle).

A U G U S T .   One reads random things in summer. Why say *one* does? I do. I read the essays of Augustine Birrell, who in his youth bought the entire works of Miss Hannah More (Holy Hannah) in nineteen large volumes bound in calf. They proved an intolerable burden, heavy in bulk, weighty in morality, with such titles as *Practical Piety, Christian Morals,* and *Moral Sketches.* What to do with Hannah More? Mr. Birrell buried the whole nineteen volumes. He dug a deep hole in his garden, stacked the books neatly, covered them lightly, and took them off his mind.

She was an Evangelical—a bluestocking who wrote Tracts—a fearful combination. But when young, Hannah More was a poet, with curly hair and big brown eyes whom David Garrick called "Nine," meaning all nine Muses in one. "Nine, you are

a Sunday woman," said Garrick fondly, forgiving her weakness
for piety and zeal.

On being presented to Dr. Johnson, Miss More said she felt
like "a worm, but a happy worm." Dr. Johnson smiled on her,
calling her "the most powerful versificatrix in the English
language." That should make anybody feel like a worm. After
such encomium she resorted to flattery and annoyed him, till
he rebuked her savagely. "Why should she flatter *me?* I can
do nothing for her. Let her carry her praise to a better market."

By happy accident she was the discoverer of "Lactilla," the
milkmaid poet. Mrs. Anne Yearsley, a Bristol milkmaid with
six children, was brought to Hannah More's attention by her
cook. Hearing in Lactilla a perfect ear, Miss More invited
Horace Walpole to read a few of her lactations. On November
13, 1784, he sent back a guarded report: "Her expressions are
more exalted than poetic. She must remember that she is a
Lactilla, not a Pastora; and is to tend real cows, not Arcadian
sheep." That, I think, silenced the milkmaid.

SEPTEMBER.   My turn came this morning to lecture
to three hundred freshmen on the short story (Faulkner) and
to undertake to pronounce Yoknapatawpha County. Last week
a young instructor named George rushed up afterward to
flatten the lecturer. "I disagreed with every syllable you
uttered," he said. "You are out of your mind!"

Today a freshman on the front row brought his lunch and
spread it over his lap: two cheese sandwiches, Coca-Cola, a
dish of vanilla ice cream. He stared enrapt, as if eating popcorn
at a movie. He gave me courage to speak my lines. "Yoknapatawpha County—" I began.

Two students walked through the hall of Carr Building
discussing a section (probably my own) of Freshman English.

"What professor did you get?" asked the one.

"Hell, I didn't get a professor," said the other. "Know what
I got? A lady!"

He sounded as upset as the six-year-old pupil who in puzzle-

ment asked his teacher, Miss Isabel Fry (sister of Roger Fry):
"Miss Fry, are you a *lady*, or just a very funny little old man?"

"The brass" are the ones in authority, the Administration.
With us they proliferate and abound: trustees, vice presidents,
provosts, assistant provosts, deans, associate deans, assistant
deans, registrars, directors of studies, chairmen of department,
plus all who sit on high-level committees, plan strategy, make
rules, pass amendments, launch campaigns for money, revise
curriculum, and are called to the inner councils to expatiate
and confer. God have mercy, does it take so many just to *run*
the place?

Brass and percussion. Sometimes I wonder whatever became
of the silver and the gold.

I suspect we prosper at home. We have bought a new roof
and a second car. I was positive I wanted a blue roof like the
roofs of Paris, Renoir blue, had always needed one, pined and
prayed for one, deprived till now. Yet when B. and I went to
look, a blue roof in North Carolina was a picture of impudence,
blasphemously blue, not only clashing with the sky but out-
doing it. My choice was a white roof on a white house, like a
white cloud sitting on a hill. B. decided on a conservative
gray. That is what we got.

He chose the second car but I chose the color, a blue Oldsmobile with the power of 375 horses. I race it down the road
like Aurora in her chariot, like riding on a besom, intent on
staying out of the ditch. In the mind's ear echoes the shocked
voice of a friend, who must have led us into this trap: *"Two*
people? With only *one* car?" The voice of America.

It was ridiculous, but as I finished my manuscript today
[When Found, Make a Verse Of], I glanced up and saw a
piece of rainbow in the sky. I was bound to view it as a good
omen, a signal from the attentive gods, till I remembered
W. H. Davies who claimed he once heard a cuckoo and saw a
rainbow at the same time. He interpreted it as heaven's
blessing, granted exclusively to him:

> A rainbow and a cuckoo's song
> May never come together again.

Yet Davies came to no good end—he lost a foot while riding freight trains in America as a tramp—that would prove the intervention of the gods in his behalf. He wrote a book, though, called *Raptures*.

The Elizabethan Woman by Carroll Camden reminds me that, at my age, a woman of Elizabeth's golden time had few expectations. She had early in life stopped dancing and trifling, had never learned to read let alone write. Only the Queen herself danced on into old age and ogled the men.

An Elizabethan saying:

> Though men are full of faults,
> Women have only two:
> Everything they say,
> And everything they do.

I like an American saying better, one to be sung by a woman dancing:

> I know my heart and I know my mind,
> And I also know I am sticking out behind.

OCTOBER. I've been reading a Profile of Susanne Langer in the *New Yorker* to find out if she deserves a place on the desert island that my daughter Peggy [David's wife] and I have set aside for wholly bearable women. Mrs. Langer is a professional philosopher whom I met years ago when she was married to the historian William Langer. Now she lives with her thoughts, without loneliness or insecurity ("The greatest security in this tumultuous world is faith in your own mind"), so entertained by solitude she will flee her house in Old Lyme and retire to a hideaway cottage to think in peace.

She might appreciate our desert island, since so far there's not a soul on it. It's a self-limiting community. Peggy and I

have considered a number of candidates, like Millicent Mac-
Intosh, president of Barnard College, mother of five, who must
be too busy to accept. We aspire to neither prophets nor carven
saints. We mean the kind of woman you would choose to live
on a desert island *with*. That rules out the shrill public women,
like Clare Luce. Miss Nancy Mitford is not in the running
(though she is said to be able to distinguish between *la
douceur de la vie* and *la dolce vita*, as well as between the
English upper and non-upper classes by their manner of
putting milk in their tea).

To mince matters, women are women and it's a wrench to
picture them on a desert island. So far, our standards are so
high in decorum, humor, and good sense we can't go to live
on it ourselves. Besides, who wants to without a man around?

Peggy and I talk also of the advantages of just staying home
and being married. She gets a copy of *Tristram Shandy* from
the shelf, with the idea of illustrating the possibility of finding
true domestic happiness in one's own bed.

Laurence Sterne praised married life and the joys thereof in
the union of Mr. and Mrs. Shandy, for whom conjugal duty
and marital accord were happily combined. They liked to mull
things over in private, as any couple should. Tristram's father,
Mr. Shandy, set aside the first Sunday night in the month and
the Saturday night preceding it to argue any momentous point
in bed with his wife. These he called his *beds of justice*—
from *lit de justice*, the throne on which the French king sat
when he attended parliament.

Addressing his wife, Mr. Shandy would open the debate:
"We should begin to think, Mrs. Shandy, of putting this boy
into breeches."

NOVEMBER. The *New Yorker* cover shows a Democrat in a voting booth, his donkey ears poking over the top,
while a queue of elephants and donkeys wait their turn. When
B. and I voted for John F. Kennedy today at the county school-
house up the road, the donkey ahead of us had ten legs—a

family of mother, father, three child Democrats herded together inside the booth.

John Kennedy sounds like a new Hotspur, fiery, young,
waspstung and impatient. He sounds tough, one of the fighting
Irish out of Boston. Through the fall he grew in stature before
our eyes, especially during four television debates. Kennedy
had honesty and wit on his side, while Nixon shrank into
mean insignificance.

Coleridge said in one of his notebooks he took no pleasure
in things contingent and transitory. "I am not certain whether
I should have seen with any emotion the mulberry tree of
Shakespeare." His choice seems to me open to caprice. Who is
to say which things in life are contingent? Or transitory?

Shakespeare had a mulberry tree that he planted in the
garden of New Place for the breeding of silk worms. It lived a
century and a half, then was cut down by a clergyman.
Thomas Sharp of Stratford bought the demolished mulberry
and made a prodigious number of relics from it, such as ink-
horns and snuffboxes. David Garrick acquired as much of the
tree as he could carry home, ordering a pretty box made and a
carved armchair. A mighty tree it must have been, fabulous
as the true Cross or the philosopher's tree itself.

But what is dull about the perimeters and peripheries of
life and literature? This is a contingent world in which I
move. I think Coleridge missed the point of Shakespeare's
mulberry tree, as significant as the little mouse under the
queen's chair.

The mulberry belongs to myth and magic. Its botanical
name, *morus*, means the fool berry (though Confucius' mother
gave birth to him in a hollow mulberry tree and Confucius was
no fool). Keats heard a nightingale one May morning under
a mulberry tree. Milton had a mulberry under his window at
Christ's, Cambridge. Children who have never seen one like
to sing and dance round the mulberry bush.

Once all mulberries were snow white. That was before
Pyramus and Thisbe, the two lovers of Babylon, killed them-

selves beneath a mulberry tree and stained the berries red
with their blood.

"Marry, our play is," says Peter Quince, "the most lamentable
comedy, and most cruel death of Pyramus and Thisby":

> Whereat, with blade, with bloody blameful blade,
> He bravely broached his boiling bloody breast;
> And Thisby, tarrying in mulberry shade,
> His dagger drew, and died.

When the Duke students chose to have a three-day lecture
series this year on "The Post-Christian Man," I said, "Post-
Christian? Why, that's me!" I informed my class in modern
poetry we would now change the name of the course to "The
Post-Christian Man," since that is presumably our subject and
our confused yet purposeful pursuit. Then I had to go and hear
the lectures.

Tonight Dr. Walter Kaufmann of the Department of Philosophy at Princeton defined a post-Christian ethic (his own).
He gave his list of four cardinal virtues, which seem not to
have changed much from yesterday's (Plato's were justice,
prudence, temperance, fortitude). The first is a combination
of humility and ambition, since humility alone is no virtue and
gets you nowhere. The second is love, not the blind love of
St. Paul that hopes all things and believes all things, but love
that accepts shortcomings and endures disappointments without dismay. Courage is the third virtue, which knows the risks
it takes. The fourth is honesty, needed in the practice of the
other three. The worst dishonesty is self-deception. Dishonesty
says, "I am doing the best I can, doing all I can."

The virtues are tested daily by encounter, and that is their
only test, through the encounters.

Having heard a wise man speak, I was simple enough to
try again, as if one might meet two in the same week. Such was
not the case. Dr. Stanley Hopper used the symbolism of
Eliot's "The Hollow Men" to cover a lack of clarity about his
own fuzzy religious state.

Worst of all, in the last hour of the meetings, a panel composed of the three speakers exploded when Dr. Will Herberg
lost his temper and bellowed from the platform. Then I saw
that, unwittingly, he was providing an encounter, one with
anger and scorn.

Dr. Kaufmann met it with no surprise. He was not dismayed
and not silenced.

Earlier, Dr. Kaufmann told a story of a man who said to
his friend, "Do you love me?"

"Yes, I love you," said the friend.

"If you love me, why is it you do not see my hurt?"

For any ethic—Christian, post-Christian, non-Christian—
the word is love.

ENCOUNTER WITH CROWS

(Heine called the Berlin of 1821 "a great crow-corner.")

Nightshadowed noon, November,
Havoc of crows and cloud
And the folly of the world,

Was meant for felicity
And a place in the light
And to be goldenboughed.

But this the *caa-aaw, caa-aaw* denies
Like an undoing word
Helplessly overheard.

I had a special regard for Will McKeever's mother, who
lived down in the hollow below our house with Beulah and
Will for the last year of her life. The day I met her I was
walking through the woods beyond my meadow. Passing
Will's house, I saw an old Negro woman standing in the doorway. She was smiling, nodding her head, hugging her body
with both thin arms. As I stopped to greet her, she burst out,
"I declare to God, I love you, honey. I love you near to death!
I declare to God above it's so!"

Taken aback by this encounter with love, after that I walked her way in case she might care to make more professions of attachment. As it happened, I never saw her again. When she died I was moved in gratitude to attend her funeral as one singled out for her love, and I went.

It was a small family funeral, thirty immediate relatives packed in the airless front room. The preacher was unacquainted, since Will's family were not churchgoing Baptists, and his remarks were pious but hollow and perfunctory. She was an old North Carolina woman who had lived and died. The compass of her life was narrow. In an attempt to wind up his oration with suitable praise and lament, he looked around the room blankly.

"Sister here," he said, "I am glad to testify was a good woman. I never had the pleasure of seeing her in church or in this life, but I know the kind of woman Sister was. One reason I know is because certain white folks are present to mourn her passing today. They thought kindly of her, which says to me our sister in Heaven was a good woman. She had some mighty good friends."

Angered by his words, I went up afterward to correct this ignorant man in his groveling. "The truth," I told him, "is the other way round. Mrs. McKeever thought kindly of *me*, and I have come to thank her." In her forgiving view, her tolerance and love, it was I who passed in this world for a good woman.

D E C E M B E R . Because I mentioned Hallmark in a verse printed in the New York *Times Book Review,* the head of that booming concern, makers of greeting cards, wrote to say (as for free advertising), "Thank you for mentioning Hallmark." Once before I mentioned Cartier in a *New Yorker* verse, quoting as a heading for the poem their advertisement: "Exquisite new gold doubleleaf clip veined with diamonds. The leaves can be worn separately—enchanting in the hair and at other vantagepoints."

"Dear Cartier," I asked,

What points had you in mind? How big
A leaf? This item comes in fig?

But no word of thanks and no diamond clip were forthcoming,
though the item cost just $3500. This is December. Couldn't
Hallmark have sent me a supply of Christmas cards?

Classes ended today in a universal shout of rejoicing, "A
shout that tore Hell's concave!" I read Milton's Nativity Hymn
to two classes, not out of Christmas sentiment but because we
had reached Milton in the course. In modern poetry we had
come to D. H. Lawrence and Edith Sitwell, two as unlikely
figures of peace and joy as the season affords. Edith Sitwell
reminds me of Chaucer's Pardoner in reverse. He preached
against the vice, avarice, he possessed. She preaches in praise
of the virtue, charity, she never had.

So I closed with Lawrence's paeon of sex ("My sex is me")
and sent them off with his message of lust to greet their
parents.

CRY NOWEL

After these autumn gales, these words that fix
Storm in the heart (like *war*, like *politics*);
After such winds of doctrine and high seas
Of worlds in controversy; after unease
And melodrama, scenes of hubble-bubble
When Vietnam enters, hand in hand with trouble—
There comes the lull. Then gladly you and I
Turn from the play, another Christopher Sly:
"An excellent piece," we murmur. "Would 'twere done."

We hurry off between the acts, like one
Retiring to look into the pewter pot
To see the world, alas, as the world's not,
To drink the frolic wine, lean out from bars
And study the front of heaven lit up by stars
From Cape Canaveral. And all is well.
Having departed from the reasonable,

The heart is warmed therefore. Nor would I see,
As Herrick said, a winter's face in thee,

This cold and frosty season of December,
A time esteemed by Chaucer, I remember,
When each rejoices loudly as he can,
And *"Nowel" cryeth every lusty man.*
So you and I, in chanson or canzone,
Cry our Nowel in that same testimony,
Devoutly in the age-old way, with—oh,
Milton's bright-harnessed angels, mistletoe,
And churchbells on our minds, still thinking of

The old words: *mercy, pity, peace,* and *love.*
For the time being, written on each face
Is Cummings' message to the human race:
"Humanity, I love you"—not, you see,
That I confuse *you* with Humanity,
But out of custom, turning back the clock,
We speak with love, instead of with Belloc:
"I wish my enemies would go to hell,
Noel! Noel! Noel! Noel! Noel!"

I bid you "Peace on earth" or send a greeting
By Hallmark to express this faint hope, meeting
Your mind thus with pure Christian sentiment
By no means hangdog but so eloquent,
So seasonable and just, a likely text,
I grieve the need to ask its meaning next—
We being a little out of touch with peace.
(*Be merry, gentle. Strangle such thoughts as these.*)
No words are hollow to the man they please.

Words to belie the winds. The customary,
Tuneful, endorsing adjectives like *merry*
We echo and exchange, a peal of bells,
Until the air is lusty with Nowels
And, on the mellowing of occasion, calm
With *peace, goodwill*—to which, without a qualm,
I add this prayerful wisdom from a note

That Madame du Deffand once lightly wrote:
"O, let us love each other." And her letter

Ended, "I do not think we could do better."
A Yule reminder, clearly. Neatly wrought.
Not only is it well put, it's well thought.
And had she written Coleridge, say, this plea
(Instead of Walpole), with sheer poetry
He might have answered in the affirmative:
"O lady, we receive but what we give."
It seems then festive to the time of year,
Like holly boughs, the running of the deer,

To speak the words we have, the really choicer
Vocables as reveler and rejoicer,
And where in books they flourish find them out
(That being what books are for, what they're about)
So that when seasons come to solace us,
I may ask meekly with Polonius,
"What do you read, my lord?" And your reply
Will show you philological as I:
"Words, words, words." This being truly said,

My simple wish is that you be well-read
And thus well-spoken, able to declare
The lashing winds but mouthfuls of fresh air,
The bittre frostës with the sleet and reyn
But words to say, in Chaucer's voice again,
"Nowel!" Six hundred years have poets spent
Harping on peace and love with the intent
Of keeping in our language, audible,
Tidings like these. And you and I as well
Still speak the English tongue. Nowel. Nowel.

1961

JANUARY. Aims for 1961 (formerly held by Horace Walpole, Chaucer's Reeve, and Wallace Stevens):

"My ambition is not to grow cross."

"To have an hoor heed and a grene tayl
As hath a leek."

"As I hope
For quiet days, fair issue, and long life."

A telephone call from Henry Simon, editor of Simon and Schuster, confirms the sweet fact we are in business. He proposes that my manuscript be in his hands by February 1, but if I wish I may delay longer, till tomorrow.

"We can wait," Henry said. "After all, poetry is eternal."

I answered so fast I stuttered: "No, sir! Verse isn't eternal, not mine. Neither is the world eternal!"

Henry agreed about the world. The deadline is left at February 1, not a mañana to spare.

We have painters in the house—house painters—who wreak havoc. The helper placed the delicate champagne glasses and the best crystal on the floor of the pantry, into which B. immediately stepped. He just opened the door and walked in. Crash. *C'est le premier pas qui coûte.*

The head painter shook his doleful head and retired to take communion and paint the bathroom, where he sings all day, "Oh, lamb of God, I come, I come."

A snowbound, freezing Friday in Washington ushered in President John F. Kennedy (my tenth President so far, and fifth Monarch, since I began life under Teddy Roosevelt and Edward VII). The ceremonies on the steps of the Capitol were marked by fateful mishaps and miseries: six inches of

25

snow, twenty-degree cold, interminable prayers by four men
of God, an expressionless store mannequin Mrs. Kennedy, a
fire breaking out on the platform to threaten all with burning.
Marian Anderson brought tears to my eyes, her magnificent
voice broken at last. Robert Frost brought tears to my eyes
as he fumbled his part in the program, a misguided, proud old
man blinded by sun and wind, trying to speak importance
when a short recitation of a poem was the most required of
him.

Well, I sighed, what will Mr. Kennedy do? Is this a portent
of griefs to come? Why isn't he wearing a coat? The President
gave us a good show, with no falter in his young determined
voice: "Ask not what your country can do for you"—it was
eloquent, you know. He saved the day.

FEBRUARY.   I mailed my manuscript to Henry Simon,
then went in a bemused state to Joan and Philip's for dinner.
The first thing their guest George Williams did over a friendly
cocktail was to call me a poetess, at which I barked my dis-
approval and glared at him. We hastily changed the subject to
dogs. I am not a poetess. I am a poeticule.

> I blunder, I bluster, I blowe, and I blother;
> I make on the one day, and I marre on the other.
>
> —John Skelton, *Magnificence*

Henry Simon wants a new title for the book. And so, by
God, do I. He wants my picture. He wants answers to a long
questionnaire, with a 200-word description of what the book is
about (as if I ever knew). He sends pages of queries ("Dear
Helen, can you find a better rhyme here?" "Dear Helen, what
in hell is this word?"), allowing me a whole week for these
trifling details.

B. says I could call it *N.B.* (*nota bene*). It will then outrival
Archibald MacLeish's *J.B.*, which is only about Job.

Phyllis McGinley says how about *Pepys Over Shoulders?*

A sailor stood on his head on the steeple of Salisbury Cathedral (whose pointed spire is the highest in England, 404 feet). For this performance his grateful king, Charles II, gave him a small remuneration—I don't know what, maybe a helmet. There's a similar story in Montaigne.

A ROYAL FABLE

A man with nothing to do—to prove or verify—
But throw a grain of millet through a needle's eye,
In time grew so unerring he was able when
Implored to by anybody to throw it through again.

At which the gentle people (they who are last to wince
At any witlessness) led him to their prince.
This man, they cried, is a marvel deserving of reward.
Their eyes were moist and shining as they advised their lord,

Who, glad to recognize how long a man must try
Before he can pass an object through a needle's eye,
Gracious to commend the piety, time, and skill it
Took—and encourage him further—
Gave him a bushel of millet.

MARCH. This morning in my office before class I reached out to pick up my book and lecture notes, to discover with cold horror I had left them at home. It was five minutes till class, home was twenty minutes away, I was lost.

I thought of Kenneth Burke, who they say opened his brief-case one morning in a classroom at Bennington College, cried out, "My God! I've forgotten my categories!" and fled back to New Jersey. What did they look like? Ham sandwiches?

Aristotle's ten categories were known as predicaments. One of them was Passion. Kant too carried his categories about with him, but I think in his head. Hazlitt tells, in the essay "On People with One Idea," of a pious follower of Kant who wore his master's categories round his neck like a pearl chain.

My category was Time (too little of) in the *Four Quartets*.
Since I couldn't run away, I walked unarmed, naked to class
and talked for fifty minutes without even a copy of the poem.
I wonder what Mr. Eliot would have done. He might have
folded his hands and said, "It means whatever it means to
you," and left hurriedly.

CATEGORIES

The mind is categorical. I could,
For instance, put into one pigeonhole
As Yeats did, *Flesh*, into another *Soul*.

I could count angels on a needle point
With half a mind and save the other part
(A solitary chamber) for the heart,

Yet hold within my head the separate stars,
Remember verse, invent myself a story,
Keep bees in still another category.

Because the mind is its own place, I could
With items of such breadth and magnitude
Fill every pigeonhole—yet think of you.

I could. O, love, how constantly I do.

B. and I drove to Cambridge, where David is teaching. And
I find it hard to explain, but I've been attending classes this
week at Harvard. The idea was to take a spring holiday. I
listened to Reuben Brower this morning on T. S. Eliot, to Jack
Sweeney in a seminar on modern poetry, and am happy to
reflect I can teach circles around them both. Mr. Brower took
the now fashionable (and fatigued) approach of belittling
Eliot. Mr. Sweeney chose an obscure poem of William Emp-
son's and left it obscurer. I enjoyed them both, but as teachers
they needed my help. (David refused to let me inside his
classroom.)
Then modesty set in. By listening to Bill Alfred, I learned in

fifty minutes how to teach. All he did was read aloud Chaucer's "Shipman's Tale." Yet he made it a lusty affair and kept a strong grip on the vowels, eloquent as John of the Golden Mouth. We students sat on the edge of our seats.

"Since Oedipus was unconscious of his crimes, it is unlikely he had an Oedipus complex." That I learned in Sweeney's class.

When Gibbon sat as a member of the House of Commons, he said of the performance: "The great speakers fill me with despair, the bad ones with terror."

Today in Boston was the Bachrach experiment. David had snapped my picture for days, since Simon and Schuster require one. These were so candid I had to put myself in the hands of a professional, trusting him to draw the line between hypocrisy and compromise.

Bachrach for Women was expert, more than that stubborn. He began by gazing awestruck into my eyes, simulating love at first sight. I smiled fondly in return, revealing my rear molars. "If you please, a little less teeth," he whispered.

He held my glance and cooed, then took forty shots before the effect wore off. Photography is like writing, which means taking forty shots. My words are not to look sloppy, nor am I. The effort must seem effortless. Hemingway wrote the ending of *A Farewell to Arms* thirty-nine times, one short of Bachrach.

"Why did you?" Hemingway was asked in an interview.

"To get the words right."

Bachrach tried to get the face right, tidied up for publication. He polished away years and anxieties, reported the subject amiable (a friend to the human race). This proved him a perfectionist and no amateur.

BACHRACH FOR WOMEN

He gazed into my eyes so tenderly
To bring out lovelight in them that I grieved
To think I had but one face to be taken,
Only one countenance to give to Bachrach.

By sighs and murmurs, moans, impassioned glances,
He sought to melt and rearrange my features
That would have daunted Gainsborough or Reynolds,
Who painted every woman beautiful—

Till we were both unhinged, unnerved, unsettled,
And spent by our emotions. "Now," he whispered,
"Smile for me, dear. Smile, with three teeth showing."
"Which three?" I panted, wondering which three.

APRIL. This is Richard Eberhart day. He is the Poet
of the Duke Arts Festival. I found myself Mr. Eberhart's
willing chaperon and daylong guide, even to a sightseeing
tour and having him unexpectedly for dinner. Somehow I never
anticipate a literary emergency by putting a turkey in the
oven. But there was ham in the refrigerator, and good red wine.
We gave him plenty of wine and he kissed me (my hobby is
collecting the salutes of the great) before hurrying off to read
his poems soberly, though when I arrived a little late I expected
to see him stretched out flat on the podium, giggling and
merry. He has a fine head for wine.

Mr. Eberhart is one of a handful of poets who follow their
profession with success in the 1960's and admit to divine inspiration. He fits the current pattern: a professor at Dartmouth
where he is poet-in-residence; Consulting Poet this year at the
Library of Congress (what do people consult poets about?);
author of *Collected Poems*, expected to win the prizes because
it is his turn; lecturer, public speaker, actor, in demand to give
readings at college arts festivals and, for posterity, make re-
cordings; a man with a sense of filling the role of Poet.

I asked him why he wrote poems about a putrid lamb with
its guts out for the crows to eat, and a dead groundhog seething
with maggots. He said, "I had death in mind."

Ann comes on Sunday morning to visit me, walking down the
dirt road by herself or with her dog Marcy on a leash. Her

mother dials my number after breakfast, but the voice I hear is Ann's. "Hello-o-o," she yells. "I'm coming!"

While I wait at this end of the road and the mockingbird sits at the tip of the pine tree racing over his notes, she starts down the hill, three years old, her tiny figure zigzagging as the big boxer noses along. It takes her five minutes to arrive, laughing. "Hello, sweetheart," I call as she approaches within sound of my voice. She shouts back, "Hello, sweetheart." Marcy is nothing but a bark.

As we walk up the driveway to my house, she stops to ask the question she asks every Sunday morning, studying me with a puzzled look. I love the grass whereon she stands. I try to reply to her in honesty, but to tell the truth I rack my mind wondering what the answer is. So we run through it again.

"Who are you?" she wants to know.

An identity problem. ("Who is it that can tell me who I am?")

"I am, let's see, I am who I am. My name is Helen. I am I. I am myself."

"Oh."

"At least I think I am."

A pause. Then she asks cautiously, "Who else?"

"I'm your grandmother."

"Oh."

"And who are you?"

She laughs. "I'm Annie."

A LAUNCHING FOR ANN

She was born in a year of marvels.
Missiles were shot at the moon
And, at her nativity,
The front of heaven was lit up
By launchings from Cape Canaveral.

It was a time when skyrockets
Took to the air like seagulls,
And at her birth the planet

Reeled to the sudden birdflight,
At last interplanetary.

It was a time of astronomers
When this earth no longer sufficed us,
And she (star-minded herself)
Became one more flying object
In space—one small bird outsoaring—

Which marks her planetesimal.

To celebrate Ann's third birthday, I gave a party for her. It
was illuminating. Not only was I reminded of what goes on at
such rituals, I was taught to survive my own. The small fry
who attended, more or less Ann's age, innocent as jelly beans,
were harrowed by the social events. A party is a hollow thing
to bear, Lord knows, but here disasters abounded and catastrophe reigned.

The big production was to be a ride on my neighbor
Howard's tractor before the ice cream. A thunderstorm struck
at the same time, soaking them through, and they crept back
into the house like whipped puppies and howled and mewled
into their mothers' laps. Then the scrapping began. Ann as
hostess entered the fray feet first till she was swept from the
room and spanked by her mother. She returned to take another
swing at cowering Elizabeth and bounce on Thomas's stomach
where he lay on the floor screaming to go home. Each child
shed large morose tears at intervals and appeared done in,
hopelessly bored, rejected, or sick. Yet at the end each turned
up a joyous face and spoke in simple gratitude, believing in
his mended heart he had had the time of his life.

Obviously I take my own parties in the wrong spirit. A little
misery is part of the occasion; one must expect to suffer despair
and the disdain of one's friends. And yet.

MAY.   The Russians celebrated May Day with a planetary
hero, Gagarin, first man in orbit. I guess he'll never write a sky

poem about the strange blue light surrounding the earth, a halo of blue between us and the pitchblackness of outer space. It's a piece of information the poets haven't had before. Above us now is space, not the gates of Heaven we used to see but the nowhere of everlasting space.

Peggy, expecting her first child, writes she is six days pregnant and already stricken by middle-name anxiety. "I think the best course is to wait to middle-name the child till she shows her dominant characteristic: Kate the Curst Bevington or Kate the Bold, Kate the Fat, Kate the Tedious, Kate the Comfortable. The problem isn't acute for boys, because she won't be a boy."

Once there was a determined Chinese lady of the ninth century named Chiang Yüan who trod on the big toe of God's footprint. God appreciated the gesture, pleased to be stepped on. By catching his attention, she asked for and got what she wanted: she wanted a child.

On the other hand, a lady of the fourteenth century made God wroth by her ill manners. In the works of Ambroise Paré, the story is told of Lady Margaret, Countess of Hagenau, who was brought to bed of 365 children by incurring God's displeasure. It happened that one day the proud countess was walking through the gate of her palace when her skirt was plucked by a kneeling beggar woman. "My good lady, give me alms."
"Why should I give you alms?" replied the haughty countess.
"Because of all the children I have begot."
The countess looked down in disdain. "Fie upon you, you've had the pleasure of begetting them."
The next year the countess was lain in with 365 children. There were 182 females, all baptized Elizabeth, 182 males, all baptized John, and one scrat, not baptized.

While filling out a recommendation for a student who wants to serve mankind by joining Mr. Kennedy's new Peace Corps, I came to the word *superb*, to be checked if it fitted the

qualifications of the applicant. Why not *peerless?* After crossing out the word, I wrote a marginal note to say I had never
met anyone in my life whom I would describe as superb. It
sounded hysterical to me. I suggested *superior* as more
probable, though not much. What is Mr. Kennedy trying to
do, give Americans a bad name?

I love Nan Cole for her way of inviting twenty people and
making each one feel that the dinner party was inspired by
him alone and held wholly in his honor. We walked in the
garden among Taylor Cole's resplendent roses and tried to be
worthy of the setting, with Scotch to help the illusion. I wore
a blue silk dress that is becoming, but I felt like a blue-
behinded ape when again somebody called me a poetess. I'm
old enough not to look clouted when accused by that mortify-
ing word. I ought to stand up to it. This is no world for she
poets.

The news of Cuba, Laos, Korea, Formosa, Pakistan, Berlin is
chilling beyond the memory of man. The planet explodes daily,
first here then there, till the state of anxiety is a twice-daily
event, morning news and night. Even if we survive the decade,
let alone the century, we'll have to admit it seemed unlikely.
Sometime, somewhere the holocaust will start.

While I teach, the world comes apart and a student writes
of Keats's "The Eve of St. Agnes" that Madeline's "azure-lidded
sleep" is a transferred epitaph.

JUNE.   B. bought me Harold Nicolson's new book *The
Age of Reason,* and I asked him if by now he hadn't given up
hope I would reach such an age. He said he had.
  When we were last in London, the *New Statesman,* which
despises everybody, spoke loftily of Sir Harold Nicolson as
"that professional human being." At first glance I took it to
be a kind of civility, meaning one officially attuned to the

human race, possessed himself of its best attributes, able to represent us in the fullest sense. Yet there was a sting in the word "professional," as of one who has lost his amateur standing.

The summer books beside my bed have grandiose titles: *The Art of Living, The Age of Reason,* and *The Nature of Love.* How to live, how to think, how to love. This doesn't mean I'm Baconian, merely a bookworm or page-eater. In the Greek Anthology, the poet Evenus says a page-eater feeds on stolen wisdom. *Ich bin Bücherwurm.*

I saw the name Robert Woods Bliss in the New York *Times* today, and it reminded me of a story I heard years ago when we lived in New York. One morning a telegram came to the Metropolitan Museum with a terse announcement that abashed the staff. It said, "Mr. Robert Woods Bliss has worms in his primitives. Please advise."

Leonard Woolf's first volume of autobiography, *Sowing,* like all the memoirs, journals, diaries, notebooks I read, makes me want to write exclusively about myself. It's an old English custom. Mr. Woolf is typically torn between confession and reticence. He is very good at being born and suckled, but after that the account steadily dwindles in excitement or intimate details. Is this all a biographer dares reveal about a *life?* Hardly an open book.

His dilemma is peculiarly British. As an Englishman who hates to walk naked, preferring to keep his pants on, he writes with a formality of style combined with a scruple for truth sometimes comical: "I remained a virgin until the age of twenty-five; the manner in which I lost my virginity in Jaffna, the Tamil town in the north of Ceylon, I will relate in a later chapter." He means in another *book.*

B. came to know Leonard Woolf in London, when the Hogarth Press published the *Memoirs of James Stephen* that B. edited. He warns me not to hold my breath awaiting that forthcoming chapter on the loss of virginity. Mr. Woolf is a mild and gentle man. He will go forth clad in chastity, like Lady Godiva.

Even light verse can reflect passion and tumult. I got stung this morning when I went out to smell the honeysuckle and smelled a bee instead. After that my nose puffed up and I spent the rest of the day writing about Pindar and the honeybees. Each line dripped self-pity, every word throbbing.

THE HONEYBEE

Just now a honeybee
Put me in mind of him
By furiously chasing me,
Convinced I had to be stung
For aspiring to honeysuckle
And honey on my tongue.

The poet Pindar, when young,
Was set upon by a swarm
Of honeybees black as a cloud
Before a summer storm,
A murmuring, threatening mass
That settled on his lips

While he lay in the grass,
And in multitudes they clung.
But the honey they left behind
Put dithyrambs in his mouth,
Panegyrics came to his mind,
And he spoke with a honeytongue.

B. telephoned from his office at 10:31 A.M. "What were you doing at 10:30?" I was down at the road looking in the mailbox.

"You went in spring and returned in summer," B. said. Summer began at 10:30. The trip was a minute long, and the seasons turned round.

When he came home at 5:00, he asked, "What did you hear on the radio?" "Not a sound," I said. He must have spent the day checking on my habits.

"Good," B. said. "Then you don't know about the escaped convict they caught with guns in our woods."

I learned when Hurricane Hazel roared like the end of the world over our heads a few years ago that the way to live through a hurricane is not to know it is one, not to know the *word* for it. Same way with tornadoes, and probably the end of the planet. It's better to think you are only in for a bad storm. Or that men are men going about their work, not escaped convicts.

The telephone rang. A Western Union operator said she had a telegram for me. I asked her to read it over the phone.

A moment passed, and another. I began to sweat. Suddenly she gave a loud shriek that tore into my ear. It scared me like a gunshot.

"Dear God, what's happened? Tell me the bad news! Quick!"

"I'm very sorry, madam," she said. "Somebody was goosing me."

The ex-Prime Minister Clement Attlee visited Chicago last week to give an address on world peace. What was next on his busy agenda, he was asked—more work for peace on earth?

"Oh, next I shall die, I expect," said Attlee pleasantly. "Seventy-eight, you know. Getting on."

J U L Y .   It's weird to write about my father and mother as if to dictation (Jules Renard: "Yes, the story I am writing exists, written in absolutely perfect fashion, some place, in the air. All I must do is find it and copy it").

Each day I learn about Charley and Lizzie by writing about them. I walk around my childhood tracing its geography, standing on our back stoop in Worcester, New York, beside the climbing cucumber vine. I am five years old. "Here I stood"—so what happened then? Why is this instant real and not another? What do I remember, and what do I forget?

In the night my mind dredges up memories to have stacked and ready for tomorrow. Often it turns up trash (orts, tares, and sweepings), presenting me with boldfaced lies, all in the spirit of cooperation. Last night I heard three words in a dream: "The cubbyhole desk!" That was the key to the mystery. That was where the secrets of my childhood waited intact to tell me who I am. Hundreds of fat little cubbyholes.

This morning my waking mind said, "Cubbyhole desk? We never had one in our house." I wish above all it were true. My mother's desk had no cubbyholes, only two small drawers. The lefthand one held a pink legal document, the divorce papers, concerning the fate of "The said female child of the plaintiff and the defendant, in their divided custody. . . ."

What am I doing anyway, trying to write prose? Verse is hard enough to keep honest. (Jules Renard: "I am afflicted with prose the way I was once afflicted with verse. When this is over, in what shall I write?")

I remember now what happened on the back stoop beside the climbing cucumber vine. It was my first experience with sex, aged five. Manley, the boy across the road, a great snickerer, stopped while we were playing house and, slyly lifting the edge of his tight pants, showed me his garter. It held up one of his black cotton stockings, as mine did. I squatted down and inspected the garter with care. It was a bit different in shape from mine but nothing special to look at, on the whole a poor exhibition.

"What is it for?" I asked politely, knowing the answer. Manley snickered.

The decade of my birth was called the Age of Optimism and the Age of Innocence, the time of the Square Deal. Aged four, I was told the end of the world had come. The year was 1910. It had already started to rain; soon a terrible flood would cover the earth, drowning everybody save for a few people chosen by God to climb a high mountain in white robes and stay alive. The news appeared on the front page of the Worcester newspaper, read aloud by Emil Meyer one Saturday morning in his tailor shop. He paused and sent a large squirt of tobacco juice into the brass spittoon at his feet.

His wife Hannah, who took care of me Saturdays while
Lizzie gave music lessons, put one knuckle on her hip to listen.
She snorted and went back to scrubbing the spots off men's
suits.

"Don't believe Emil half the time," she said, grinning at me.
"He likes to read the funny papers."

I wasn't afraid if she wasn't. But I regret that even in the
Age of Innocence the world was no safe harbor for the human
race. As early as 1910 the planet threatened to disappear
under water.

THE CHILD IN THE PHOTOGRAPH

"What have you in common with the child of five whose photograph
your mother keeps on the mantelpiece? Nothing, except that you happen
to be the same person." —George Orwell

The mother has tied her hair with a white taffeta bow
Like a butterfly on her head,
Which gives her a comical air of being exhibited,
A docile child on show.
I have no idea though what to make of her. If only
She'd smile. If she weren't so small
And tractable. If only with less transparence
She were visible at all.

If only I might leave her alone on the mantelshelf,
Let her be meek and five,
No longer care, or believe, that she is myself,
Or even real or alive,
I think I might recognize easily at a glance
What has more relevance—
A familiar look or other deeper in her eyes
Than obedience to her mother.

A U G U S T .   Virgilia Peterson's autobiography, *A Matter
of Life and Death,* is motivated by hate, an emotion for which
I have no respect. She addresses her mother in cold fury as

"you," an evil woman, and is herself touched by pitch. This is a self-wounding book with no healing in it, no cure, filled with revenge, the desire to hurt and destroy a dead woman.

It is perilous to tell an honest story in the first person. It is dangerous to write about one's life, in a book one may bitterly regret like committing a felony. Am I doing that? I am not writing with hate.

My mother Lizzie was strait-laced and genteel, Victorian, cherishing her good name that she would, if necessary, not hesitate to lie to keep. She was respected and loved in the small village of Worcester. These were her best years when she held her head high after the scandal of the divorce from Charley—the Methodist preacher caught in adultery. She dared anyone, as she said, to "cast a slur."

If I hadn't peeked out from bed one night and seen her passionately kissing her suitor Mr. Peckham, who aspired to become my next father, I shouldn't have thought all my life she knew how to kiss. Had he tried to put his hand on her breast as they sat on the couch, he would have felt a ruffle. She would never allow such "liberties."

She weighed about 108 and, except for no bosom, had a good figure with a neat waist (tinier if she had drawn in her corset laces). Her hair was lovely, dark brown, shiny. It made a heavy braid down her back at night. She was pretty as a picture, though she hated having her picture taken. And I claimed her. I trusted her. She was mine, I was hers.

It annoyed her to be teased for having the same name as the Tin Lizzie. She ate sugar on cantelope, watermelon, tomatoes, fried oysters, and fried eggs, and so did I. On her birthday when I was five, I gave her a dozen oranges and a box of ZuZu ginger snaps.

Lizzie spanked me often, having to be both father and mother, with no man in the house to straighten me out when I cut a dido. Though jammed full of fears, I knew my mother was not. She feared nothing and said so, boasting she could take care of the two of us, taunting imaginary men, drunk or sober—men who were mashers, cowards, coarse-mouthed womanchasers. I was warned against men, little boys, beer, the

Pope, and running about on Sunday. Lizzie lashed out at life when it needed a beating, or tore into any threat to her respectability and floored it. When I came down with chicken pox, she diagnosed bedbugs and turned the whole house into the front yard while she searched and scrubbed for an entire day inside. Her face was grim with the shame of it. Then Mrs. Preston from across the road dropped in to take a look at my bites and said "Chicken pox."

My father Charley revealed aloud his anxieties and terrors, aware of his mortality, beseeching God to save him. Why wouldn't life give Charley Smith what he deserved? Why had he been overlooked? Born for success, with his quick mind, his wit, possessed of charm, such available talents, well, it was this way as my mother told me, "He always destroyed what he gave." "He was like a milk cow," she said, "that gave you a pailful of cream and then kicked over the bucket."

Women became his mistresses, men his cronies. A natty dresser, a sporting man, he liked saloons, prizefights, racetracks, smoky rooms, but not indecent stories or tarts. Charley the preacher owned a sleek racehorse and challenged anybody he met to a buggy race, clipping down the dirt road of Main Street, laughing, shouting, winning. When he abandoned us one night and took the train for New York, leaving us behind, he left behind his horse and a huge bulldog named Bully in honor of Teddy Roosevelt. Lizzie gave them both away.

With his belief that women are inferior, meant only for marriage, what could Charley do with a daughter? I was Lizzie's child, her hard luck. Yet there was his occasional guilt. Sporadically he made amends by sending costly gifts: a boy's Indian costume with chief's headdress, an oversized bicycle, a carton of horehound candy. I grew used to hating their arrival. Charley was almost a stranger. "He is your father," Lizzie would say, as if admitting to a crime. "It's a good thing you've got me."

After he married Addie six years later and went to live in Binghamton, a hundred miles away, he felt obliged to have me, aged eight, on his hands for a visit. The prospect upset him, the sight of me filled him with remorse and wore on his nerves. Life sent these miserable trials, and I gave him heartburn.

During the six weeks I was there, I slept with Addie during the first three weeks and with Charley, at the other end of the upstairs hall, for the last three. It must have been some penance of Charley's. I accepted my lot and did as I was told. Since I had always slept with my mother, it seemed natural to sleep with somebody. But I preferred Addie. Charley groaned and snored.

Just before he sent me home in August, Charley took me aside and gave me a lecture. His stern blue eyes held mine. "Now, listen carefully, Helen. I want you to use your head and remember this. You are never, understand, never to tell anyone you slept in the same bed with your father. Do you hear?"

"Yes," I said.

"Yes what?"

"Yes, I won't tell."

"Your mother wouldn't like it, but that's the way she is, prudish. People are funny. They see wrongdoing where there is no wrong. You get the picture? Keep this to yourself. Promise me, Helen."

"Yes."

And I kept my promise. I wouldn't have told my mother on him in any case. Far be it from me to rouse her to rage, as I sensed it certainly would. She would have laced into him. She would have had a conniption fit.

Wherever Charley lived in his roving life, he bought space in the local cemetery, for himself and as many loved ones as he could count at the time. Sometimes he bought a tombstone as well, which said SMITH. Since he moved often, he acquired reservations all around the country: five plots in the state of Maryland, three in Worcester, New York, a hillside in Sidney, New York (where he proposed to lie beside his parents), in Waverly (where now Lizzie lies alone), in Binghamton. On arrival in Chicago, he bought up a whole corner of six plots in the Bohemian Cemetery, to be sure of a place next his beloved Addie. It was the only real estate he owned. A restless, rootless

Charley wanted to be assured his piece of earth. Charley the landowner.

But, little or much as I've inherited of my father's nature, it is not a taste for graveyards. My feeling about them is like that of Dylan Thomas's Grandpa (in *Portrait of the Artist as a Young Dog*): "Grandpa paused at the churchyard and pointed over the iron gate at the angelic headstones and the poor wooden crosses. 'There's no sense in lying there,' he said."

I went once as a child to a revival meeting with Lizzie to hear the evangelist Billy Sunday (an earlier, more theatrical Billy Graham). I took alarm at the way he yelled at God and wrestled with the devil, whipping about the stage, leaping to the pulpit to thump the Bible, falling to his knees and bursting into tears. He wound up as if throwing a baseball and shouted at me "Repent!" But Lizzie shook her head not to pay any attention. Nobody ordered her around.

Afterward, when she told me Charley had been an evangelist, I was ashamed. How could Charley save a person's soul? She said he sang gospel songs, a singing evangelist, and the congregation loved him. He was a hit. Even so, I was ashamed for my father.

Lizzie had a dream, one that filled her nights for many dark years with longing and intermittent hope. And it became my dream.

When my mother had eloped with the young singing evangelist Charley Smith, in a wild impulse she could never account for, she lost Will Hovey. The photographs she kept all her life of Will (I have them now) show him a blackhaired, blackeyed, laughing undergraduate at Cornell, to whom she had been engaged for a year before she met Charley. Will had a passion for photography. He took pictures of the two of them, on picnics and on Sunday, first setting his camera on a tripod, tripping the timer, and leaping to his place beside Elizabeth (he never called her Lizzie), so that in the poses he comes out looking breathless, his straw hat on the back of his head, his cheek close to hers. She looks young, proud, happy in her starched shirtwaist and long skirt, a small loop of ribbon in her hair. There's no doubt she was in love with Will Hovey. And I was in love with Will Hovey. It was a lesson she taught me. Besides, I had eyes to see what I too had lost.

Lizzie's mother died when she was eighteen, and the Hoveys took her in as their own daughter. She stayed most of the time at their house in Waverly, New York, because she was Will's girl and Will's sister Kate had been since childhood her closest friend. It was a love match, wholly approved by my widowed grandfather John Raymond. Will was the man for Lizzie: the gods should have seen to that. He would have given her his love, his life, his children (not me, of course). I was a poor return for the happiness she never found.

She eloped with Charley in March of Will's senior year in college, three months before the date set for their wedding. On hearing the news from John Raymond, Mr. Hovey took the next train for Ithaca to tell Will himself. He feared what desperate thing Will might do (so my mother explained it to me). When she and Charley returned to Waverly six years later, in disgrace after his scandalous affair with a married woman in Maryland that had cost him his pulpit, the Hoveys had moved away, to the Upstate town of Lockport. She heard no word of Will, nothing, and she was too ashamed to ask.

Then I was born, and my parents went to the tiny village of Worcester, where Charley preached in the Methodist Church till another scandal with a woman brought an end to that. Their marriage had failed, their tragic little drama acted out before a population of a few hundred. My parents were divorced when I was two. Because of Charley, Lizzie had become estranged from her father. Because of Charley, she was left with me to support. It was in Worcester when I was five that I first began to hear about Will Hovey.

Lizzie, who had become a music teacher, chose that summer to go to Cornell (Will's school) to study public-school music. That summer she was reunited with her father, John Raymond in Waverly, only a few days before he died, killed in a train accident. During our brief stay in his house, he gave her distressing news of the Hoveys: Kate had died in childbirth; Will, now a lawyer in New York, had married his secretary but was separated from her; Mrs. Hovey, grieving till she cried her eyes out (Lizzie told me), had become totally blind. One thing she asked in her blindness was that she might see Elizabeth once again.

So began our visits to the Hoveys in Lockport, three or four times a year till Mrs. Hovey died. We couldn't go to her funeral, since Will would be there—he never knew of our visits to his parents. I may have been twelve when we stopped going. We would take the Erie train of a Saturday morning, my mother and I, and spend the weekend in a large gloomy house where Mrs. Hovey sat out the day on a black horsechair sofa in the parlor with the draperies closed. My mother sat with her, and they talked of Kate and Will while Mrs. Hovey wept. Her weeping terrified me. What would happen to her pale wet eyes when by now she had cried them away? She was a small plump woman with white hair and trembling hands. She would run her fingers like mice over my face, then drop her hands to her lap, leaning again toward my mother. And she would say, "How I wish she might have been Will's daughter."

Will had a daughter, the same age as I. While the women talked, I spent my life poring over the album of photographs Will had taken of his child. We were six when I made her acquaintance in this way—Virginia, forever Virginia, on the deck of a ship going to Europe, Virginia in Central Park with her father (his cheek close to hers), Virginia in white fur coat and muff, Virginia on a Shetland pony, lucky Virginia laughing beside her governess—Will Hovey's daughter Virginia. She was rich, the happiest girl in the world. I studied her, envied her, learned her by heart, resented her for taking my place. On each visit I asked to see the book, bulging with more and more pictures (but none of her mother), so many that they were no longer pasted in: Virginia with her chums in a private school on the Hudson, Virginia in a silk party dress and long black curls. Then the photographs stopped.

When she was ten years old, Virginia was stricken, rushed to a New York hospital where they found she had bone cancer.

They cut off her right leg above the knee. A few months later
they cut off one arm at the elbow. The next time my mother
and I visited the Hoveys Virginia was dead. It was our last
stay in that house. When his wife died, Mr. Hovey, a silent old
gentleman in the coal business, lived on alone with the house-
keeper to look after him. He never asked us to come back.
Perhaps he hadn't wanted us at all.

The end of the dream, Lizzie's and mine, came shortly after
my own marriage. On a holiday trip by car that summer to
Thousand Islands, I was sitting beside B. studying the map of
upper New York State when my finger stopped at a familiar
name. "Lockport!" I said. "There's Lockport. Look, it's right
on our way."

"What of it?" B. said.

We had brought Lizzie with us. I turned to her. "Wouldn't
you like to see the old Hovey place one more time?"

She shook her head. No, oh no. Then she hesitated. "If we
could just drive by—"

We had trouble finding the street and the house, whose
address eluded us. Obediently, B. drove past. It appeared less
stately than I remembered, otherwise the same gloomy brick
house. At the end of the block, B. circled around and came
slowly back. As we passed the second time, a man opened the
front door and stepped out, pausing on the porch. I had never
in my life seen him before, but I knew his face better than my
own father's. "Stop, please stop the car," I said. It was Will
Hovey.

When I jumped out, he came down the walk to meet us. My
mother hadn't moved. He glanced past me, at her through the
car window. "Elizabeth, it's Elizabeth!" he cried and, opening
the door, held out both hands. She seemed unable to speak. It
took much urging from Will and even more from me before she
agreed to go with him into the house, while B. and I followed
behind. Will brought out some sherry. There Lizzie sat like a
stone on Mrs. Hovey's sofa, her hat hiding her face, saying not
a word. Will and B. began a lively conversation, taking to
each other like old friends. Because of his father's recent death,
Will was staying to settle the estate, give up the house. He

would leave in a day or two. "Thank God," he said, "I shan't ever return to this place, not now."

I stared at him. This was Will Hovey, just as my mother had told me, just as I wanted him to be. I loved him. I belonged to him. He was good, he was wonderful, a striking man with dark hair not yet gray, taller than Charley and kinder, with a low reassuring voice, a warm smile. He seemed eager to talk and to listen. I had a great deal to tell him, the unhappy story of Lizzie and me, the way it happened, the way it was. He might be shocked and appalled, he might be sorry. Or he might understand. I had to let him know.

As the minutes passed, Will moved his chair close to mine, calling me Helen. Several times he touched my hand, smiling, trying to bring me into the talk. At each attempt I heard myself making a reply so brash it sounded rude, making a fool of myself. The topics were wrong, they were absurd—golf! Will liked golf for relaxation, to which B. agreed. I said I hated it, that B. tried once to teach me and I *hated* it. When Will mentioned politics, since he was now in Washington, I said I voted Socialist and closed that subject like the click of a box. B. looked startled at my remarks. Once he frowned as if to say, pull yourself together.

But my mind raced to find the right words before it was too late. What on earth could I say to him, and how should I begin? Should I blurt it out: "Mr. Hovey, all my life I've wanted you for my father"? (I, a grown woman.) "Mr. Hovey, at last I've found you—it must be fate—" "Mr. Hovey, will you listen carefully, please? The truth is I wanted to be Virginia. I wanted to *be* your Virginia, your daughter. You see, I loved you, we loved you, my mother and I—"

B. glanced at his watch, time to go. The visit had lasted a half hour. We four went in silent file down the walk, and at the car door my mother said a quick goodbye to him. I heard my mother say, "I wish you knew her, Will."

"I wish I did," Will said. "After all, she's your child, Elizabeth."

As we drove away, he stood at the curb watching us. I didn't look back to wave goodbye, nor did Lizzie huddled beside me. I was crying too hard.

SEPTEMBER. Now we have a Berlin Wall. The sudden closing of the border between East and West Germany was an act of Ulbricht's. But it was Khrushchev who gave the order from Moscow: 40,000 East German soldiers and police, using tanks, trucks, barbed wire entanglements, sealed off East Berlin to prevent flight to a free world. Hitler built a wall around the Warsaw ghetto to destroy a people, and the Jews died inside. This is a wall of bricks and concrete to divide two worlds. How can you keep a *world* walled in? They are finding a way, by watch towers, gun implacements, a mined death strip, searchlights, ferocious killer dogs. It is inhuman, insane, a Wall of Shame, but there it is. A wave or nod to a friend across the barrier is forbidden to East Berliners. Anyone trying to escape is shot on sight. The specter of World War III walks again.

"Under the trees two men and two women were sitting around a tea table, all of them presenting the kind of appearance, more common then than now, that suggests that nothing untoward ever happens to the human race."
—Rebecca West, "Parthenope"

The leading editorial in today's New York *Times* speaks of the nuclear blasts in Russia. The Soviets have resumed nuclear testing in the atmosphere, and soon will we—a bombarded planet threatening human beings alive and yet unborn. This is sixteen years after Hiroshima. "It is the heart of all humanity that should be heavy. . . . It is as though man, the aspiring, aiming at the stars, should suddenly reveal himself as no more after all than the uncouth beast of the primordial slime."

Next to these horrifying words is a piece about Monarch butterflies, now in September emerging bright as day lilies, starting their annual trip south. "Sometimes they travel single file in streams that reach for miles. Sometimes they go in flocks like sunset-colored clouds." You would think a poet wrote that. They should be passing overhead, not bombs but butterflies, on their way to Florida for a winter in the sun.

I walk into my garden. Above the marigolds hovers a

Monarch butterfly, elegant in orange wings with black veins
and borders—very regal, very consoling. It's supposed to have
a spicy odor like sandalwood.
"Read not the *Times*," said Thoreau. "Read the *Eternities*."

In the old days, what comparable drama did newspapers
find to write about? From H. R. Fox Bourne, *British Newspapers:* "For lack of fresher matter, the Leicester *Journal* in
1752 reprinted by instalments the Book of Genesis."

We had a Faculty Women's Cocktail Party this Saturday
afternoon, an official and historic occasion given by Miss
Frances Brown (professor of chemistry) to launch women on
the primrose path. A coven of eighty librarians, deans, house
mothers, and teachers, each a female, gathered to drink
Manhattans and martinis together and drown care, an awesome
spectacle of moral disintegration. A husband was heard to say
as he deposited his wife at the door, "Did you ever in your life
hear of a *women's* cocktail party?"
We moved in determined sobriety, "the very pineapple of
politeness" to quote Mrs. Malaprop, in tableaux and minuets,
four hands round and on to the next. It was a brave gesture,
but my belief is that women don't take to each other in groups,
don't mellow under the influence of strong liquor. Nobody
kindled and was lit.
Still, it's a hope for the future that might be bottled and kept.

Lizzie misunderstands my antiquarian interest in the past,
her past and mine. She sends me a box of my baby clothes all
ribbons and lace, embroidered by her with rosebuds and kept
folded away in a box with my pink booties and a lock of
blonde hair. There is a white silk dress and bonnet that Victoria
might have worn, how sheer and fragile now. They put me in
mind of mummy wrappings. I have as much use for them too.
Yet the book I'm writing may look, to my children, like these
sentimental shreds, yellowed baby things, better forgotten. I
ought to burn the manuscript in the fireplace before the ghost
walks.

My neighbor Howard says his mother saved everything the
way Lizzie does. His mother made little cloth bags to hold
pieces of string, each bag carefully labeled as to the length of
the pieces. After her death they found one small bag of string
labeled "Too short to save."

OCTOBER.   I wish I could read a book, not to be
written in my lifetime, *The History of Poetry in the Atomic
Age*, or *The Rise and Fall of Poetry*—a book that will reveal
whether poetry managed to survive and last out the century,
or went straight to the dogs.

It will say how the poetic revolution came out, the counter-
revolution, and the counter-counter revolution, who won or
lost the war of words, which rebels and activists were shot,
what Prufrocks lay by the roadside. In a century of wars,
poetry has fought its bloody own in the thick of battle. At this
dismal moment, the conqueror seems to be prose. But some
future historian will name the two or three poets who lived
through it; will marvel at *The Waste Land*, probably ask,
"What did the people in that collapsing world learn from the
chaos of *The Cantos*?" Already from the University of California comes the rattle of computers as the *Cantos* are tabu-
lated on IBM punch cards. It takes a machine to shake down
that poem.

Were I to read tomorrow's textbook, I wouldn't believe it.
It will have a perspective not mine, reflecting the calm ruth-
lessness of time. And it will lack something—the quaking in
my bones shared by the poets who speak the rhythm of my
world.

If a group of these poets were collected in a single volume,
a gathering of the hellgazers—Day Lewis's *Overtures to
Death*, Eliot's *Waste Land*, Pound's *Cantos*, Auden's *Age of
Anxiety*, Ginsberg's *Howl*—they would add up to a monstrous
indictment. And would the picture be honest? Not entirely:
incredible but close.

It might dismay less, though, than an anthology of contemporary poets, who write hellgazing poems about dead pigs,
lambs, cats, toads, woodchucks, and fish; poems called "How
to Eat An Orange," "Paring the Apple," "Peeling Onions";
poems about getting a haircut, using a vacuum cleaner, stepping on a beetle, scrubbing a potato, hating a housefly ("O
hideous little bat, the size of snot")—poems that avoid the
grander themes of terror or joy, poems by the fly killers.

NOVEMBER.   Francis Brown, editor of the New York
Times Book Review, invites me to write another holiday verse
for the front page of the review, to appear in December. I
love to be asked, love him for asking. When he makes a
hurried request like this, with some preposterous suggestion
and a deadline two weeks away, I say, "Yes, Mr. Brown." This
one makes me laugh and hang my head. It's the holy limit,
the final folly—forty lines on the subject of *paperbacks.* For
Christmas?

It's hopeless. I can't do it but I will anyway. Is there anything
poetic about paperbacks?

In despair I ask B. what the devil I am to do about such an
idea for verse, and he says, "Do what the Muse told Sir Philip
Sidney." (*"Fool! look in thy heart, and write."*)

THE HAPPY READER

Thou sittest at another book
Tyl fully daswed ys thy look
—"The House of Fame"

"What learning is!" cries Juliet's Nurse (I with her)
Had we but time for learning. Who has time?
Who listens in this giddy world to wise men?
Who now reads Plato or Plotinus? I'm
Only inquiring, yet with every bookstore
These parlous days heaped to the rafters high

In paperbacks, no doubt the simple answer
Is *everybody*. Even you and I.
For where the volumes flourish, then the readers
Must read betimes and turn to read again,
While books come tumbling out the skies like buttered
Larks that once fed the people of Cockaigne.

Or do we buy to give away like emeralds
These lavish texts and titles, old and new?
These Dantes, Miltons, books of hell or heaven
From Paradise to *paradis perdu*,
These Shakespeares, Sartres, myths and bestiaries,
Bibles, rare bibelots, old almanacs,
The Works of early, mid, and late Victorians
(How lovely life is, full of paperbacks).
We read them in the rain, perhaps, these Homers,
Find them in guest rooms—Montaigne, Molière—
Learn words of love from all the better poets,
So many ways to read a book are there.

Or if a taste for mingling with rejoicers
Is yours and mine, the Wife of Bath comes now
In paper covers, who survived five husbands.
Or Falstaff makes his *jest with a sad brow*.
What can we lose to walk with such companions?
Secure from the hobgoblins of the mind,
Distracted from dubiety, safe as readers,
Wiser to leave a little care behind;
Well-educated, say, like Henry Adams
And, like Micawber, happy to possess
Not capital but talent for enjoyment,
Knowing we can afford allknowingness.

For paperbacks are like Mohammed's angel
With 70,000 heads, each separate head
With 70,000 faces, each face speaking
With mouths, each mouth with tongues, and (so it's said)
Each tongue delivering truth. On this vain planet
Whenever it behooves us, you and me,

To learn Cro-Magnon ways, or Christian ethics,
Or how to play the trombone, fortunately
The item is at hand among booksellers,
Where cure for every ignorance may be found.
The rest is only leather and prunella,
And life is lovely, being paperbound.

D E C E M B E R .   I attended the Campus Club luncheon
in a hat. There were 250 other hats present, each hat so large
this year it overshadowed and hid from sight the lady beneath.
From the speaker's table my hat rose on signal to address
the rest.

Of a sudden I remembered an academic dinner a few years
ago at Duke when a lady professor got up to speak ("Up roos
the sonne, and up roos Emelye"). She was toastmaster at the
annual banquet of the Erasmus Club, a learned society to
which we English teachers belong.

"Let us now be lusty!" she rose and cried, clapping her
hands.

There was an embarrassed silence. While she looked ex-
pectant, the members smiled nervously and dropped their eyes.
Nobody knew where to begin or really what in the world
to do.

So I spoke (lusty as a cockcrow) for twenty minutes in the
dozing part of the afternoon. I said one way to pass the time
was to keep a notebook for making a note in, after which they
applauded and gave me two Wedgwood vases and a bouquet
of flowers. The difference between ladies and students is that
ladies are gratified by what they hear but do not take notes.
Professors do not take notes and are not gratified.

Next morning the Durham paper quoted me as using *like*
as a conjunction and splitting an infinitive. It said I was a small
woman who wore a hat as an afterthought—with an elfin look.

"Such were her thoughts, but she kept them to herself, and
put on her bonnet in patient discontent." *—Northanger Abbey*

Henry Simon sent me for Christmas a leatherbound copy of *When Found, Make a Verse Of.* It is a pretty book, a very pretty book. I don't like it. The binding abashes, too rich and lavish for my words. Who would guess a person would object to being done up in giftbook purple morocco?

1962

JANUARY. Always begin the new year with a new typewriter ribbon and a robust heart. I feel safer with the even years, though odd numbers are more mystical. "There is a divinity in odd numbers," said Falstaff.

That was true last year. John Braine, the angry young author of *Room at the Top*, prophesied the immediate end of the world. "There will not be a 1962." Now he says he slipped a digit.

When the telephone rings, the breath stops, with a child about to be born. Yet I can't phone each night to Charlottesville, where David now teaches, and say, "What's new?" Surely when my children were born I had no sense of a waiting, breathless world. Charley sent a silver dollar both times, and my stern grandmother Smith wrote, "Call him Enough."

David took Peggy to a Danny Kaye movie and urged her not to laugh for fear he would have to remove her to the hospital before the picture ended. He has been timing her contractions, which he claims occur two days, 9 hours, and 23 minutes apart.

A child was born, but it wasn't Kate. It was Stephen. David phoned as if to speak immortal words from the Shakespeare he teaches: *A bairn, a pretty bairn. A boy or a child, I wonder?* It's Stephen, born male, stark belly naked to the world, a member of the wedding. I called my mother to tell of her new great-grandchild.

"My *grand*child," she corrected me. At 87, that is as far as she will go, not to be saddled with greatness. To defeat old age, she skips a generation.

R. P. Lister, in a poem "Pinkerfly," inquires the whereabouts of that infant born of the operatic union of Lieutenant Pinkerton and Poor Butterfly. "What came of infant Butter-Pinker-

ton?" he asks. "Grew he from Pinkerchild to Butterman? What
was the future of young Pinkerfly?"

Half white, half yellow, like a tiny tent,
Who picked him up and whither was he sent?

In Puccini's opera, Butterfly called the child Trouble.

FEBRUARY.   I wonder about the Wonders of the
World. When Mausolus, king of Caria, died in 353 B.C., his
widow Artemisia, loving him, built him a splendid mausoleum
at Halicarnassus, and it became a Seventh Wonder (Philon of
Byzantium saw all seven about 146 B.C., and declared them
wonderful). It stood 140 feet high with 36 marble columns,
above which rose a flat-topped pyramid with Mausolus in a
chariot drawn by four horses, a lovely woman beside him
(Artemisia, no doubt). Though the sepulchre survived some
1500 years, no sign of it remains.

I'm baffled, though, to read that each night at dinner
Artemisia took a pinch of her husband's ashes in her wine, till
finally she had drunk him up. By thus imbibing him, she
claimed she had become his living tomb. Two years after his
death she died.

Who, then, *did* occupy the mausoleum of Mausolus? Artemisia? If she came to repose there, as seems appropriate, she
must have been a tomb within a tomb.

John Aubrey says, "Dead Men's bones burnt to ashes and
putt into drinke doe intoxicate exceedingly."

What about the Seven Horrors of the World—the Monstros-
ities, the monuments to bad taste? Like the seven sins, they
would be more likely to survive. (How long does a Wonder
last? Nine days, they say. Or so.) I can recall being stunned
by three or four Horrors, all contemporary. The Prince Albert
Memorial and the Brighton Pavilion. The gilded equestrian
monument in Rome of Victor Emmanuel under his mustaches.
The statue at Thermopylae of a Spartan warrior clad only in

a helmet and poised to hurl at the Persians a lance so remark-
ably long it would never clear the narrow Pass. I also nominate
the Corn Palace of Mitchell, South Dakota, whose immense
exterior is covered with thousands of bushels of corn, the
kernels arranged into mosaics, red, yellow, white, blue, of
American pioneers, Indians, and bison. Rising skyward are
bulbous towers, minarets, and onion spires crowned with
American flags. Each year the palace is attacked by corn
borers and has to be restored. The borers are its best critics.

Ruskin, who had a keen eye for Horrors, went one day to
the Kensington Museum, "and there I saw the most perfectly
and roundly ill-done thing which, as yet, in my whole life, I
ever saw produced by art. It had a tablet on front of it, bearing
this inscription:—

Statue in black and white marble, a Newfoundland Dog standing
on a Serpent, which rests on a marble cushion, the pedestal orna-
mented with pietra dura fruits in relief.—*English. Present Century.*
No. I.

It was so very right for me, the Kensington people having
been good enough to number it 'I,' the thing itself being almost
incredible in its one-ness . . . so absolutely and exquisitely
miscreant, that I am not myself capable of conceiving a
Number two, or three, or any rivalship or association with it
whatsoever."

B. and I attended a "fallout" meeting today, a new and
frightful kind of discussion group. At least it didn't mean we
were falling out with each other. It was held in a wellmeaning
spirit of paternalism at Duke to acquaint us with the present
perils and consider plans for sheltering us, to prolong life a
little, in case of atomic attack.

If there is a direct hit on this city, the leaders explained, no
plan of action is contemplated. It won't be necessary. It will
be too late. One may participate in the holocaust as an innocent
bystander. But if, say, Washington, D.C. should be the target,
or the nuclear installations at Oak Ridge, Tennessee, we might

have an hour's grace to decide whether to hide ourselves underground for a couple of weeks, thence to emerge to whatever life or lack of life remained on the surface.

Duke has some winding tunnels beneath the University now being studied as refuge, though the problem of ventilation is not solved, nor the more embarrassing question of who is to be allowed inside and who (rated non-academic) rejected at the door. Without air, I doubt that it matters.

Even so, the plan is more humane than the gas ovens at Buchenwald or Belsen. It would be a more impersonal hate that destroyed us. One's crime would be not that one was a Jew but that one was a human being.

M A R C H .   John Ciardi talked tonight at Duke on "The Poet and Society." He appeared not in the least foiled by the expansive title.

As a poet he is against hate, given or received. He is against pressures and power structures. He is 100% for freedom, especially for Ciardi. When they made him a professor at Rutgers, he resigned and fled to escape capture. What matters if you are a poet is to write a poem. You put everything second to that—society, God, love, sex, money in the bank, and a partridge in a pear tree.

Ciardi says the FBI has him listed, in his attitude toward America, as "foolish but loyal." That describes pretty well, I think, his attitude toward poetry.

Matisse said, "I wish to be remembered as a living man." The words have upset me all day. Who would want to be remembered as a dead man?

Matisse also said, "L'oeuvre est paradis" (it sounds better in French). I can well believe that.

Gertrude Stein had a maid, Hélène, who did not like Matisse. He would stay unexpectedly to a meal, asking beforehand what there was for dinner. So when Miss Stein said to her,

"Monsieur Matisse is staying for dinner this evening," she would say, "In that case I will not make an *omelette* but fry the eggs. It takes the same number of eggs and the same amount of butter but it shows less respect, and he will understand."

—*The Autobiography of Alice B. Toklas*

It is the tone of voice I want to change. Why sound indignant, why scornful? Whatever the fault (a student hasn't read the assignment), it has happened a thousand times before. I grow tired of caring, bored with my impatience.

Iris Origo in the *Atlantic* tells of asking George Santayana in his old age whether there were many things he would like to change. No, he said. "I feel I have much the same things to say—but I wish to say them in a different tone of voice."

In the second century A.D. Athenaeus, a grammarian, wrote *The Deipnosophists in* fifteen books, whose title makes my jaw ache. It's about 29 philosophers at dinner who make bright remarks and tell amusing anecdotes. I'm glad to have missed the banquet, where you can hear the snores of the listeners. I've snored my way through Athenaeus. Yet how else would I know the story of the happy people of Tiryns?

They were full of laughter. Unquenchable. They laughed from morning till night, till their lack of sobriety began to seem excessive and worry them, and they felt ashamed of themselves. They went to the oracle at Delphi to ask how to subdue their mirth and become decently grave.

Apollo answered they must sacrifice a bull to Poseidon by casting it into the sea without a smile. To execute this painful task, the people of Tiryns eliminated, as too playful, all children from the ceremony. Just as they were throwing out the bull, a little boy slipped into the group and cried, "What's the matter? Are you afraid I'll drown your victim?"

At that the whole populace burst into roars of laughter. So they were punished. They remained the merriest of Greeks, guilty of laughter, to which they resigned themselves and went on laughing.

Lord Chesterfield to his son: "How low and unbecoming a thing laughing is: not to mention the disagreeable noise that it makes, and the shocking distortion of the face."

B. stopped at the A. & P. on his way home from school.
"I saw Taylor Cole in the store," he said. "I had a long and fascinating talk with him [the Provost] about pansies."
"Is it a serious administrative problem?" I asked.
"Pansies," B. said. "They come in little boxes." And he handed me three purple pansy plants from the A. & P.

A P R I L .   My mother Lizzie arrived at Easter, 600 miles by Trailways bus which she prefers to airplanes because it takes longer. Her straw hat had a pink rose standing up in front. Before meeting this 87-year-old great-grandmother, whom she had never seen, Ann asked, "Will her face be black?"
    Recently my mother needed to have the leaky roof repaired on her tall two-storey house. She hired a neighbor, an amateur carpenter, then chased up the ladder after him to tell him how to fix it. They spent most of a week on its steep sides together, Lizzie climbing up and down to keep a sharp eye on him.
    "It was a funny thing," she said. "His wife grew suspicious."
    "Of what?" I asked.
    "Of me. She was jealous."
    "Oh, come."
    "It's as true as I live," my mother said, well pleased. "She didn't like what was going on up there at all!"

We talk of my childhood in Worcester. I try to think of hundreds of questions to put to her, then am amazed that she knows the answers. By now I seem to have invented the town, the people, herself and myself. But she knows better, and I say, like the Wife of Bath, "Aha, by God, I have my tale again!"

David had the following conversation with William Faulkner in Charlottesville, where Faulkner now lives and David teaches. They met head on at the door of the library of the University of Virginia.

"Excuse me, sir," said David, backing away.

"After you, sir," said Faulkner, backing away.

"Thank you, sir," said David, forging ahead.

"Thank *you*, sir," said Faulkner, crashing into him.

I record this interesting exchange for future biographers, notably as a study in Southern courtesy for historians of the novel.

(1966. C. M. Bowra in his autobiography *Memories* reports an encounter in his youth with the great Henry James. James, surveying him, asked politely if the young man was still in school. "I replied that I was." End of anecdote.)

"I am not a professional writer," Peter Taylor began this afternoon. "I don't think of myself that way." And he read to a group of us a fetching story called "Demons" from his childhood. I found it exciting, so much so that afterward I asked if this was an interweaving of invention and memory, or only (as I hoped) memory. He said it was strictly the former, meant to be read as fiction, a short story.

It was about hearing voices as a child. One voice said to him, "Ruin. Ruin." Another voice spoke as he was sitting on the toilet, in the tones of their kindly colored cook, "Are you going to sit on that Christmas tree all day?"

But the story puzzles and confuses me. Which parts did he invent? Why wasn't the truth enough? I keep thinking how I want to *understand* the past, not create it. I want to know it unadorned, the way it looked. Peter could have used his art of storytelling to say what really happened. He didn't want to.

M A Y . Doris Lessing calls it "lying nostalgia," making stories out of one's life. I ask myself, even with truth the aim, is she right? What is gained in the end? Shape. An arrangement of events. A clarity of pattern, though that is what life lacked in the first place.

So one lies. It didn't progress in logical fashion. It wasn't even plausible. The events occurred but not in the sequence one devises with each day leading to the next. (Dylan Thomas: "The memories of childhood have no order and no end.") At best the mind keeps a few isolated scenes, fragments unwoven into past or future, tatters to make into a fabric. I could write a dozen versions.

Yet why not make sense of my life? I can learn nothing by leaving it unwritten, blurred, disorderly. If I contrive the links, call it dishonest, but at least methodical. Neat.

Or one could write a bestiary. Or a cookbook.

A garden party at President Hart's summoned the faculty. We were asked on arrival, "Where is your station?" (B. and I didn't have one). Various elected people were dotted about as points of welcome. A busy couple stood beside a step in the flagstone walk to catch ·bemused professors as they plunged headlong. A mark of distinction is to be invited to pour the strawberry sherbet, with shifts every half-hour to pass the privilege around. A lady so honored wears no hat.

While my chairman's wife stood at the punch bowl, she said to a professor at her elbow, "I'm sorry, I don't believe I know your name."

"Never mind the name, girl," he snorted. "Just hop to it and serve up the glop."

There is this element of risk in being taken for the help.

At the closing exercises of Mrs. Twaddell's school, Ann was graduated from Pre-Kindergarten I to Pre-Kindergarten II, dressed as a pussycat. Because she can carry a tune, she was assigned to lead her group in the song and dance they have practiced for months. She also has a one-track mind that tells her to dispose of one item at a time. Her opening performance was to stalk to the front of the platform, raise her hand to her brow, and more Pocahontas than pussycat scan the horizon to locate her family. The teacher had to yank her into line where she executed her dance in a fitful fashion, coming to a dead stop each time round the circle, with the whole group of twenty stacked up behind her, to conduct another search. We sat

frantically waving an umbrella that the show might proceed.
I was falling off my chair with laughter.

Afterward we said, "How did it go, Ann?"

"I was good," she said.

J U N E .   Leonard Woolf has published his second volume
of autobiography, *Growing*, about going out at 24 to Ceylon
in the Ceylon Civil Service, taking with him 90 volumes of
Voltaire and a dog named Charles. (Byron had a set of
Voltaire in 92 volumes.)

As I feared, the loss of his virginity didn't amount to much.
Seems he was riding gently down the main street of Jaffna
when he caught sight of a Burgher girl on her verandah. She
smiled, he smiled. Soon after, a small boy trotted beside his
horse. "Sah! Sah! That young girl ask whether she come to
your bungalow tonight."

"I very foolishly said yes," says Woolf, "and she came and
spent the night with me."

Definitely not worth waiting a year to learn about. He didn't
even say why it was foolish. In my opinion it wasn't. Had he
said No, I would have had another year to wait for the
next book.

Mr. Woolf enlarged this confession by the following state-
ment: "I have always been greatly attracted by the undiluted
female mind, as well as by the female body." (I can't figure out
what the Burgher girl did to reveal her mind.)

Undiluted. Well. One of the endless charms writers possess
is their persistence in using the wrong words. Christina
Rossetti, for example (and she a poet), in "O love songs
gurgling from a hundred throats" made a sound like the drain
in the kitchen sink. Marvell wrote the phrase "My vegetable
love" that seemed right and accurate till somebody punctuated
it in a London newspaper: "My vegetable, love, should grow/
Vaster than empires and more slow."

Robert Frost introduced two wrong words in a single line of
a poem when he described "The peeper's silver croak." There

is nothing silver about a croak. Besides, peepers peep, as Frost the Vermont farmer well knew, peeping high and shrill approximately two octaves above middle C to say it's time to make love. (Christopher Morley thought they sounded like sleighbells, which is closer than a croak.)

Gerard Manley Hopkins wrote of the skylark, "Why, hear him, hear him babble and drop down to his nest." Idiots babble. Or babies. Or brooks. Not birds.

John Crowe Ransom began a stanza of "Philomela," "I pernoctated with the Oxford students once." Not knowing the word or any Latin, my students don't dare to think what kind of orgy Ransom was up to at Oxford. It means to spend the night, preferably in prayer or vigil. Ransom listened to a nightingale.

Ruskin took strong objection to the line "The spendthrift crocus with its cup of gold," since the crocus, anyone knows, he said, is not spendthrift and its color is saffron. It has no gold to spend.

The wrong word is like a sore thumb, too painful to ignore. There is the posturing word that prances into a sentence calling attention to itself. Isak Dinesen boasted of three things she did better than average: cook, take care of mad people, and write. *Mad* people, the sentence stopper, the rift in the lute. Why must they be mad? (Cheshire cat to Alice: "We're all mad. I'm mad. You're mad.") Yet to heap praise on Isak Dinesen, Eudora Welty said she possessed a seraphic mind, in itself a toplofty word. Who has a seraphic mind? A lady who takes care of mad people.

These days, it's the pornographic word, the four-letter Henry Miller word, obscenely dull, that diminishes the vocabulary to Basic Non-English, the kind of word, said Eliot, "not fitted for the company in which it finds itself."

Jules Renard observed in his Journal, "If the word *cul* [backside, bottom] appears in a sentence, even in a sublime sentence, the public will hear only that one word." And he chose the wanton word *cul!* He died in 1910.

What bad luck it was for poetry when the noun *pants* came to mean a pair of drawers or britches.

On barren mountains doth Adonis lie
A boar's white tusk hath gored his whiter thigh:
His short *pants* Venus grieve . . .
—Bion, *Lament for Adonis*

Leap thou, attire and all,
Through proof of harness to my heart, and there
Ride on the *pants* triumphing.
—Shakespeare, *Antony and Cleopatra*

Make love's quick *pants* in Desdemona's arms.
—*Othello*

[Ottima, speaking to her paramour Sebald:]
Sebald, as we lay,
Rising and falling only with our *pants*,
Who said, "Let death come now!" . . . Who said that?
—Browning, *Pippa Passes*

Again and again Jules Renard saw the problem facing him
of writing words, using them honestly. "Every moment my pen
drops because I tell myself: 'What I am writing here is not
true.'" Then caught in a lie he tried again: "Do not say that
what I write is not true. Everything is true; say that I have
written it badly."

Gilbert White of Selborne had by nature a courtesy with
words. He was a little formal and courtly in manner but never
pompous, never vain, the essence of civility. The style was the
gentleman, a reader of Horace, a lover of lapwings.

In a letter to Thomas Pennant, he wrote: "On a retrospect,
I observe that my long letter carries with it a quaint and
magisterial air, and is very sententious. . . ." (This was after
he had told engagingly of the warble of the blackcap, the song
of the redstart, the wailing note of the flycatcher, the sound of
the whitethroat.) "But when I recollect that you requested
stricture and anecdote, I hope you will pardon the didactic
manner."

To read him is to find one's manners mended.

J U L Y .   Montaigne took care to explain himself, but he never wrote the story of his life. "This is the way men are," he said, accepting his condition of being a man but failing to include in his essays such women as his mother, wife, and only child, Léonor.

James Anthony Froude's autobiography, which I'm reading, also passes over the females in his family, his three sisters, without praise or blame or even comment. His four brothers are identified as real people; the girls merely have names— Margaret, Phillis, Mary. But surely he loved them. Didn't their voices sound in his ear as he wrote? Weren't they under the same roof, a part of him?

Froude's own life was a matter of ordeal, profit and loss. He was endlessly absorbed by its drama and the role he played. Like John Stuart Mill he wrote in defense of women, arguing for the equality of the sexes, for the personality of the individual. Yet of the year 1836, when he was eighteen, besides mentioning the death of his eldest brother Hurrell which was a shattering loss, he records as an afterthought—in three words—"Two sisters died."

A U G U S T .   B. and I drove up Highway 15 the 600 miles to visit my mother Lizzie in Hornell, N.Y., past the green pines of Virginia and the Gold Mine Pentecostal Holiness Church. Till recently on these trips North, we hurried to cross the Mason-Dixon Line to the Yankee side, then took a deep breath of Northern air. Now we look with love at signs pointing South, where the time is standard, the traffic light, the climate kind, the place home.

Twenty miles before Gettysburg, wham! the ballyhoo begins. As loyal Americans approaching a national shrine, we are commanded to pray at a replica of the Grotto of Lourdes, dine at the Battlefield Diner, drink beer and dance, play miniature golf, and take up bowling. For us Jungleland awaits (a snake farm of cobras and pythons), an Indian village, a Church of God, and the Civil War for sale—flags, toy cannons, busts of Abraham Lincoln in imitation bronze, postcards of the Gettysburg Address. We have a choice of handmade bedspreads, hooked rugs, or Stuckey's nut butter crunch, pecan clusters, cocoanut patties, divinity fudge.

The Civil War Museum is advertised next door to Howard Johnson's. We may sleep at the Battlefield Motel with AAA rating, the Lincoln Motor Lodge, the Mason-Dixon Inn, Blue and Grey Cabins, or the Battlefield Trailer Camp. But we hurry on, past the battlefield itself—thirty square miles of it— to be viewed, had we time, from a helicopter or toured in an airconditioned bus equipped with stereophonic sound to reproduce the shouts of Pickett's Charge, the ear-splitting screams of cannonballs. A three-day battle rages daily at Gettysburg.

And in the hot summer sun the cornfields shine with their crop of great gray monuments.

THE ROAD TO GETTYSBURG

Consider the journey now, on Route 15,
In rolling country—the valleys and hardwood hills,
The sky like summer as it has always been,
The same neat farms, the fences, the red barns (these
Ayrshire cows in the meadows), and everywhere
Along the highway still the apple trees.

But the changes? Naturally they had to come
In time, in all that time, with none to say
The way it looked or what this is different from.
So consider the journey now. Of course it's more
Commemorative than when my great-grandfather
Traveled this road in July once before—

With bunting, flags, memorials, Blue and Grey
Cabins for tourists, Battlefield Motels,
A Grotto of Lourdes in case you want to pray;
With diners, fruitstands, filling stations near
The place itself (half-hidden by monuments),
And everywhere for sale the souvenir.

Maybe the only difference is, one has
More proof and witness now, more signs to pass
Like Stuckey's Chocolate Pecans or Mobilgas
Before arriving there. But there one sees
The same green fields that other terrible journey
On this road led to, past the apple trees.

Just before the New York State line, in Covington, Pa.,
there's a tavern where we stop to fortify ourselves with a beer
before reaching my mother's teetotal doorstep. We've carried
on a running conversation for years with the bartender about
wild turkeys.

"Let's see, you're the turkey hunters from North Carolina,"
he says with a grin, recognizing us. He is a deer-and-bear man
himself.

Neither B. nor I have seen a wild turkey in our lives, or
looked for one, but B. has shot a couple of woodchucks. To hold
his end up, he tells how you track down a turkey by strewing
wild rice in its path, having mastered, like Defoe, the art of
"grave and imperturbable lying."

I come to see Lizzie, who thrives, with a new heart interest
(before it was Bernarr Macfadden, the health faddist with the
bulging muscles. Now it's Lawrence Welk, who waltzes on
television and has sent her his picture). She takes Geritol.
Lizzie has longevity by the tail. Battered but unscathed by
time and misfortune, she has plenty of failings of which the
unfaltering ability to survive is not one.

I come to walk the streets of my childhood, in case they're
still there waiting for me to write of them. We moved to
Hornell in 1914. The same cats walk Bennett Street, the same
elms heave the sidewalks. I peer cautiously into the eyes of
passing women, the baggy-eyed ones, plump around the middle; they may be former schoolmates. So far I've run into Miss
Thatcher, the librarian, in a pink hat. She says she is 88 but
looks younger by half than when I was a child. Books have
preserved her person and her sanity. The hundreds of books
that passed between us like a handshake have made us friends.

"You used to be a Reader," she says to me. "In the old days, people were literate. Tell me, my dear, do you still read?"

BENNETT STREET

My street is long in shadows long
As time is long and if I cry
No one will hear me passing by
Where every windowshade is drawn
The people in the rooms are gone
As time is gone and none will hear
My footsteps, none will guess my fear
And say "Is it some child we know?"
And shake their heads and let me go
Down the longshadowed sidewalks down
Down Remember Street, my own
Heart racing down the night alone.

S E P T E M B E R .   Another poet is dead, E. E. Cummings. Living or dead, lower-case or capitals, a poet makes a mortal difference in my life. If he lives, the pattern of his world, even his identity, may change. He may raise hell's roof, causing me no end of trouble. If he dies the scene is set and unalterable. In either case, I must rewrite my lecture notes.

Add *fl.* to his name; he flourished. He found his way of being alive, then finished the pursuit. Hundreds of my students will grieve because they loved him for staying young and saying *yes* ("yes is the only living thing"), for believing in love, for spending hours over a semicolon because he liked semicolons.

"Gladliness is next to godliness," he said, to be ungladly is a crime against the gods. (Or, the proverb says, *C'est plus qu'un crime; c'est une faute.*)

I hope he died like Cézanne, whom he praised for "the most fortunate and illustrious of deaths, at the *motif*, in the execution of his art." Cézanne died after working as usual outdoors at his easel. A violent storm came up and he hurried away, falling in the road where he was found and carried home in a cart.

I saw two poets tonight on television: W. H. Auden and Richard Wilbur. B. would have chosen to go on watching a murder mystery—not that he objects to poetry, far from it, only to modern poets. I saw Auden in the flesh twenty-three years ago at Columbia University, when he looked untidy. At present he looks like a ruin. Is it from too many gins or too many couplets? And how volubly he talks, interrupting his interviewer Walter Kerr, stating his answers with more finality than an answer requires: *this* is what poetry is (play or magic), *this* is how it is written (by lovers of words like Auden). You would think anyone so often spectacularly wrong—about life, love, poetry, women, the human predicament—would be less confident in his delivery. How can he make so much *announcement?*

My favorite couplet of Auden's (from *The Double Man*) is one I am sure he didn't mean, except ironically:

And Woman, passive as in dreams,
Redeems, redeems, redeems, redeems.

Still, he was livelier than Richard Wilbur, who chanted his poems in hushed tones, lifting his voice to set the words afloat, treating his lines with breathless awe regardless of their sense. He read his charming poem "Love Calls Us to the Things of This World" as if he had no idea what it was about. It is about laundry (looking like souls without their bodies), hanging fresh and clean on the clothesline:

Outside the open window
The morning air is all awash with angels.

Some are in bedsheets, some in blouses, some in smocks—clean innocent pure souls swelling in the breeze, flying in space.

Why should a man of wit speak words not for their meaning but solemnly, for the poetical effect? He looks witty.

"And what to say of him, God knows." One must proceed cautiously with poets.

_____

I am spinning the story of Charley my father out of my own
guts. It is not like a silkworm spinning undoubted silk, or a
spider spinning a web to catch its dinner. It is like a woolly
worm spinning all cry and no wool. I am kneedeep in my
commonplaces.

How could I ever *invent* Charley? A preposterous man.

If only I could remember how risible he was. "Ha, ha, *ha!*"
he roared at his own jokes and doubled me up, the funniest
man. I hear his laughter, not his words. But in his black moods,
yes, I know well enough the curses he howled then.

Elizabeth Bowen said about her Dublin childhood, it is not
a matter of memory. It is a matter of reliving. Henry James,
more chary, returned to a "visitable" past. I hear the many
tones of Charley's voice, I see his face; yet how much could a
child of eight really understand?

What would I think of him now?

Peggy in her delightful spelling writes that Stephen is being
weened. Not overweened? No. Stephen sounds like Henry VIII,
bold and "weening in his pride."

O C T O B E R .   President Kennedy spoke over television
at six o'clock tonight (October 22) on the decision to blockade
Cuba. It was clear: war or peace, stark, intensely urgent. Russia
is bringing atomic weapons and missiles into Cuba to aid
Castro. "The greatest danger of all would be to do nothing."

Adlai Stevenson addressed the United Nations to say what
we, unlike the Communists, see as threat to survival. The
crisis is extreme, the danger chilling. Cuba is ninety miles
away.

Bertrand Russell cabled both heads of government not to
start a nuclear war. He said, "We'll all be dead in a week."

While drinking coffee with friends, I heard the testing of
airraid sirens and (in a state of nerves) cried out, "This is it!"
Twenty years ago in New York, B. and I heard the sirens of
World War II when a German bombing attack seemed about
to begin over the city. "This is it!" we cried.

NOVEMBER.   Lizzie is dying of cancer. I sit beside
her bed in Hornell's Bethesda Hospital, recalling how often
she has said, "Nobody can fool me"—a trumpeted claim, a
boast, a warning to all who would deceive her. Now she is
able to fool herself. She does not, cannot, face the reality of
death.

Dr. Pullman told me this morning my mother will live no
longer than a week. I think he is wrong, though I have never
seen anyone die. She is what indomitable means. Her will is
strong, she is unyielding, a fighter by instinct. When I told her
B. would fly to Hornell a week from Wednesday for Thanks-
giving, she said, "Good. I'll be home and well before then."
For her this is better than resignation. At first I didn't think
so, heartsick that she wouldn't ask what ailed her. I couldn't
conceive of such self-delusion. Now I hope she will die
believing she will live.

While my mother sleeps under sedation, I go for refuge to
the Hornell Public Library. My God, what a ghost I have
become. The place hasn't changed since I was eight years old.
It is impossibly the same, musty with sameness. The books I
once read are where they were on the shelves (Edna Ferber's
Roast Beef Medium, Poe's *The Fall of the House of Usher*).
While still in grade school, I used to meet Dick secretly in the
children's section on Sunday afternoons. In high school, Harold
and I held hands in the history section to the left of the main
desk. Murray and I read love poems in a shadowy kissing
corner at the right; he taught me one thing a book is good for.
I certainly kept busy on Sunday afternoons.

Since the present librarian is a sourpuss, I haven't asked if
the Pink Shelf of erotic books survives hidden behind the
office door. But then I no longer delight in pink books.

The fact my own books are in this library seems fanciful but
unimportant. It might have pleased me at the age of eight, if
such an ambition had occurred to me. I think it never crossed
my mind.

Lizzie cannot turn over in bed. She cannot eat. Her face is
a tight knot of pain. Yet she tells me confidently she is better,

since the way to get well is to be better each time one asks. I am grateful to her for not giving an inch—at last I am grateful. I look at her suffering and see my own probable fate, death by cancer, a condition she would never accept. And I tell myself, "I shall not be fooled."

But I think, these long nights, of death and of my lost childhood with my mother. Even as she is dying, I am writing clotted words about her, late into the night when I return to her house from the hospital. It is the only way I know to meet my grief.

Strangely I'm haunted, comforted, by a story told by Po Chü-i, poet of the ninth century, who at forty had a daughter named Golden Bells. When she grew to be one year old, he wrote a poem about the trouble of getting her married. At the age of three, Golden Bells suddenly died.

> By thought and reason I drove the pain away. . . .
> And three times winter has changed to spring.
> This morning, for a little, the old grief came back,
> Because, in the road, I met her foster-nurse.

By this time Po Chü-i was the father of a second daughter, whom he named Little Summer Dress. When she in turn became three years old, he wrote a poem about her:

> But all the world is bound by love's ties;
> Why did I think that I alone should escape?

DECEMBER.   My mother died Tuesday night at 6:30, and it was a bitter death for me. She couldn't say how it was for her, speechless and I hope unaware, though I do not know. I only know she was determined not to die, didn't *want* to die, wasn't tired of living in spite of fifty years of solitude. She had no deathbed scene in mind after five weeks of pain in hospital. They said she would ask for help in good time, at least help for her soul, but she never asked. She talked no nonsense about death or eternity. She died valiant, with courage and honor, true to herself.

This Saturday morning we closed her door and drove away from Hornell, B. and I. Lizzie's house is as she left it, every piece of furniture in place, full of her possessions. I am no collector. I shall sell it as it is, remember it so, with her own grape jelly in the refrigerator. I pray never to return.

Yet each middle of the night I wake still in her house and can't find the way home. In a nightmare—or is it hallucination?—I hear her voice at the front door calling "Helen!"

In this fast-disappearing year I lost a mother and gained Stephen. I lost another year of my life, lost to grief, gained love. I learned a ternarie of littles: a little life is better than death. A little peace is better than fury. A little hope is better than fear.

1963

JANUARY. This is a winter journey. And this is our sabbatical leave, taken together, B.'s and mine. Yesterday the New York harbor was choked with ice, some of it in my heart. My first feelings on a ship or plane are claustrophobic, the more fool I to risk the journey. As we sailed at teatime yesterday, the gold windows of the golden city gleamed from every skyscraper, while two strangers confided to us over a teacup their First-Class status—how many furs left behind, how many world cruises taken. One said her suite was too cramped, so expensive does she come, so rich and plaintive a lady.

The *Vulcania* is rich too, ornate like a fine old bawdy house, done in dark mahogany, rococo gold-fretted panels, mirrors, Raphael cherubs, a naked marble lady in the dining saloon. Our cabin has a glassed-in verandah, to which I opened the door a crack and shuddered at the bleak sea. This morning in the Gulf Stream, turned toward the Mediterranean, the passengers are thawed out. A charming old person from Montreal, Dr. Archambault, asked me if by chance I taught at Duke University.

"But how extraordinary! What a coincidence!" he exclaimed. "Only a moment ago I conversed with an intelligent man who also teaches at Duke."

"That is her husband!" said his wife sharply in French.

I'd like to meet some porpoises, in case they are happier than human beings and, as is said, have a sense of humor. Still, I have a dry body unavailable to porpoises, and an Italian table steward bending over me with a slice of Persian melon: "Would madame care for a piece of this lovely fresh meadow?" Porpoises do not dine on caviar, lobster thermidor, capon, and champagne, nor do they dance the twist till midnight, while the Captain never misses a whirl on the dance floor and the *Vulcania* sails uncommanded on the black windwhipped sea.

75

What if the boat had sunk last night before we were assigned lifeboat stations? Lined up for boat drill this morning like First-Class sausages (a baby sausage in its mother's arms), we acted bored silly with this child's play. Yet a man behind me remarked, "I was shipwrecked wearing one of these when our ship broke in two. Spent ten hours in the Atlantic and lived." He was in the war, or a war, some war. Our Italian bartender was a POW, World War II, confined at Camp Butner a few miles from my home.

I love the sea; in my family tree is the Keeper of the Eddystone Light (who slept with a mermaid one fine night). I lie idle in the sun while the other passengers take Italian lessons after breakfast. What good is Italian in Greece? I wish I had brought along Harold Nicolson's *Journey to Java* to remind me how at seventy he worked eight hours a day in his cabin, surrounded by reference books, examining his contentment, pursuing at sea the question of causeless melancholy. In the end he concluded there is no such thing. I could have told him that. A cause or two always exists, like sloth or the lack of an interesting aim in life. (He forgot to say so, but the phrase appears in Wordsworth's poem of 1802, "To H. C.," "O vain and causeless melancholy!") It took him six months coming and going to settle the matter, all the while remaining happier than in this world he ought, free of causeless melancholy.

Tonight we attended a small cocktail party graced by a purple-breasted Anglican bishop and his lady. He was a meek, old-fashioned man (I mean he drank old-fashioneds) with a benign face. His lady, which a bishop marries instead of a wife, came larger, with a jutting bosom and a piercing voice. After one martini, she vowed to all present she wouldn't kiss the Pope's hand or foot. Nobody had asked what her view on the Pope was, which anyhow lacked urgency, but it engaged her mind. In mid-ocean I hadn't thought what to do in case the Pope walked upon the waters and presented himself—prob bly go ahead and kiss.

Madame Archambault collects curios. She has a curio collection at home in Montreal of miniature objects from her travels: tiny china slippers, bits of lapis lazuli, glass flowers. I too collect curios: I collect Madame Archambault. She looks like a tiny librarian and has the energy of an Alpine climber. In camel's hair coat and tan beret, she charges around the promenade deck, ticking off the miles. At the fortieth time round, she stops at my deckchair to speak in her over-precise English.

"One cannot rest. One has boundless zèle. Do not let me dismay you, lying there prostrate with your book."

Our table steward, Aldo, entertains us with an occasional joke. Recently he told his wife in Trieste, when she reached the age of fifty: "I will now turn you in for two lovely girls, each 25 years old."

I stare at him amazed. Does he know Byron, in *Don Juan,* quoting the lady Donna Julia wedded to a man of fifty?

And yet, I think, instead of such a ONE
'Twere better to have TWO of five-and-twenty.

Where did Aldo learn that? Was it first a big Italian joke, current in Venice in 1818? Aldo can barely speak English.

FEBRUARY.   Today, February 1, we reached Lisbon. One cold winter night in London, B. and I saw a film "Lovers at Lisbon" with Trevor Howard, spies and intrigue. I said then, "To hell with Portugal. This is London." Yet Byron wrote, "What beauties doth Lisboa first unfold!" Henry Fielding took a voyage to Lisbon to die.

At 4:00 P.M. beneath hundreds of circling gulls and a double rainbow curved over us like a suspension bridge of prisms, we made our procession, while people went on drinking tea and children played in the *Saletta bambini.* I can't take a rainbow calmly. In sunshine and rain, past red roofs and gleaming white houses of Estoril, we followed the green Tagus River into the port of Lisbon. What an entrance!

Tonight in town with the Letchworths—an American couple from the ship—we stood uncertainly in a downtown square, wondering where to find a nightclub, café, streetcorner, or bar to hear native Fado singing. Fourteen university students crowded around us to point the way to wherever we would go, but nobody understood our pronunciation of Fado. A passerby, a sweet Portuguese lady, stopped to listen and smile. Without ado she summoned a taxi, ushered us into it, gave directions to the driver, and waved goodbye.

"This place I send you is not chic," she said. "It is simply the best."

The long ride took us back to the ship, down by the docks in old Lisbon, a sinister neighborhood. At the shadowed door of *A Cesária*, we were greeted by the whole family—mother, daughter, two grown sons, small grandson, none of whom spoke English—and beckoned into a narrow empty room lit by a lantern and one dim gas lamp. It was only 9:30, too early for the night's entertainment. The place with its few rough wooden tables and bare floor looked a picture of poverty.

The sadfaced mother in a ravelled sweater over her shabby black dress hurried to bring us a pitcher of wine. She stood beside our table and began to sing, her voice low, beautiful, full of anguish. She was followed one after the other by her daughter, a son, and a stray visitor. Two guitarists arrived and sat down directly in front of us, picking up the accompaniment.

It was Fado song, passionate, mournful lament, bittersweet and heartbroken, like Edith Piaf's wail over unhappy loves but more wrenching and enthralling than hers. They say the words are often improvised out of grief. It told of the doom of love. You knew that by listening.

Slowly the room filled with Portuguese natives, who ate spicy sausages cooked at their tables over an open flame and drank huge pitchers of vino. We stayed most of the night, unwilling to leave this family, who followed us to the door, wrung our hands and kissed them wordlessly. "Happy," I said, "hap-py." It was the happiest night I had spent in years. The rainbow had done its work.

Our taciturn guide to Lisbon, John, spoke in short declarative sentences: "The view is delicious." "The entrance is freedom"— motioning us to enter Our Lady of the Mountain overlooking Lisbon and the harbor. "The time is not much."

Two black-shawled women bustled about, dressing a statue of the Virgin in real cloth garments, shielding her body from our glances as they threw over her head a well-fitting white-and-gold gown and many gold necklaces. Her pretty hair was real, a wig of winsome brown curls tumbling down her neck. She looked demure, stylish, a wax model in a store window, a sweetfaced manikin.

"They prepare our Lady," said John softly, crossing himself. The Virgin smiled.

On Sunday morning it rained in Casablanca. This glittering city of Morocco basks in the blazing sun for 336 days of the Mohammedan year. For us it rained, in the dark time of Ramadan and tears.

Lucky's real name was Bousmara M'Hammed, a plump laughing Arab with shabby clothes and goldfilled teeth. "Is everybody happy? Lucky wants everybody to be happy." As tour conductor of Bus #4, he taught us Morocco in one day's easy lesson.

"Morocco is democrat country," he began, no trace of irony in his voice. Only the rich pay income tax. The poor have no income. We drove to the European section, its spacious streets lined with date palms and pepper trees, its balconied villas festooned with yellow bougainvillea, its bloom tropical, its wealth obvious. "How lucky we are," said Lucky, "to live in Casablanca!"

In a few moments we were in the five-hundred-year-old Casbah, where the beggars lay out asleep in the rain. Veiled women in ragged burnooses, bearded old men with angry eyes, ragged children wandered in filth and squalor. They stared sullen or spat and turned away. At the Arab market in the old Medina, a place to bargain for old brass, bronze, silver, the merchants sat at their prayers with averted eyes, ignoring us. The rain grew to a downpour, then a deluge.

For shelter Lucky took us to the Marhabar, a luxury hotel

in the modern city, where as tourists from a cruise ship we
were offered free drinks, a choice of champagne or Coca-Cola.
My countrymen without hesitation chose Coca-Cola. Lucky
walked among us laughing, *"C'est la vie!* Happy New Year!"
though for him it was Ramadan, a time of fasting and prayer
when, Mohammed said, the devil's leg is chained and the door
of heaven open. As we climbed aboard the bus, someone asked
if he liked Americans. He sat down to deliver his reply through
the microphone, a born spieler.

"We are brother, we are sister, democrat country like you.
In Morocco we are in the same leaky boat. Life is not much,
comme ci, comme ça, with equality for all, Arab, European,
Jew, all equal, all free. So far it's a pretty good dream." He
laughed, shrugged. A fat chance. "Is everybody happy? Lucky
wants everybody happy."

On the Mediterranean, from my deckchair I follow John
Steinbeck's *Travels with Charley,* an absurd journey compared
with mine. He crossed America in a rumbling truck com-
panioned by a French poodle with bladder trouble (a less
lovable hero than my Charley). He put up with hardship,
loneliness, fended for himself and Charley, lost his way,
scrounged for food, moaned in self-pity to get the damned
journey over and write his book. What did he learn? "Each
man is alone on his journey."

Two Siamese cats in first class have traveled around the
world two and a half times. They have rounded the Cape of
Good Hope, Lord knows why. They are surly, bored, hissing
in disgust, closing their weary eyes like some of the other
passengers.

"Do you see this stick, sir," said a man once to Sydney
Smith. "This stick has been around the world."

"Indeed," said Smith, "and yet it is only a stick."

Palma de Majorca lay outstretched, curved about the harbor
like a beach girl longlegged and golden in the sun. She looked
distinctly Côte d'Azur, pink with flowering almonds, cerulean
of sky, shining with olive trees.

The ship's captain recommended life on Majorca by citing

the sexual life of Errol Flynn, who lived at Palma with count-
less mistresses and a yacht. No word was said of George Sand
and Chopin, how they lived, loved, and made ends meet. The
passengers were aquiver at the name of Errol Flynn.

Nothing came of so promising a start. We were whisked off
to a thirteenth-century cathedral facing the waterfront and
shown a collection of relics, one a small rough piece of wood
imbedded in a gold cross heavy with jewels. "A piece of the
truly cross," said the guide, his eyes reverent, never revealing
the miracle—how this poor splinter found its way from
Calvary.

I studied a bony finger of St. Theodosia and an unidentifiable
piece of St. Stephen, holy but gruesome. I read once in the
World Almanac that St. Stephen's right hand is on show in
Budapest; he must be scattered all over Europe. In Padua is
preserved St. Antony of Padua's tongue. If it can speak, so
much the better.

Before we reached Sicily this afternoon, the Inglises gave a
large luncheon for their most intimate friends of nearly two
weeks. It takes only that long on a ship to form undying
attachments.

I sat beside a man to whom I didn't yet feel intimately
attached, not having laid eyes on him before. But the outlook
was hopeful. When I murmured "Peace" over my sherry, a
ritual to help save the planet, my companion echoed "Peace."
If everyone in the world said the word daily, he reflected, the
sound would be always in the air—like a white dove bending
its wings over us, crying *Peace, peace.*

While the band played "Deep in the Heart of Texas," we
docked at Palermo and roared away in a bus straight to
Monreale, climbing the royal mountain up heights of cactus
and rock as the moon came out. On the pinnacle rose a town
of twenty thousand, and a twelfth-century Arab-Norman cathedral. This we had come to see.

Inside, we groped in darkness. So suddenly that a woman
screamed, a thousand lights were turned on. Two tons of gold
gleamed in our eyes from gold-inlaid mosaics covering walls
and ceiling—gold, gold, blinding gold in an exquisite radiance.

The tremendous Christ above our heads had the stern face of an Arab, lifting two fingers to bless instead of the Roman three. A dark passion shone on his suffering face, an awful grief achieved long ago by the patient fitting together of tiny irregular pieces of stone.

A twelfth-century Margaret of Navarre lay buried in the cathedral, with scampering white marble rabbits set into the floor at her tomb. They were meant to compliment the submissive wife of William the Bad, mother of William the Good. Who would want to be praised for eternity as a timid white rabbit?

On the autostrada to Pompeii, going south beside Vesuvius, I thought the volcano looked safe with heavy snow on top. It had erupted, though, since last I saw it; its contours were changed. Pompeii, only fifteen miles from Naples, lay prostrate at the foot of Vesuvius. Till now, I hadn't realized how near the destroyer was, right overhead behind the Forum. So it had looked to the Pompeiians, harmless and safe. The killer bided its time, deceptive with snow.

One readily peopled the square with brightrobed citizens of twenty centuries ago, the fat Romans carried along in litters. Life never ended in Pompeii. A day was interrupted, held intact—the figure of a fallen boy outlined in molten lava, a dog still writhing. Modest the baker had left fresh loaves in his oven, each loaf stamped with his name (immodest Modest). The sky might have fallen yesterday. It might fall today. Why not?

The rich Romans lived at the westend of town, among them two bachelor brothers, the Vettiis, in a luxurious villa. They lived with a decadent air at the Casa de Vettii, in love with the flesh that proved so mortal. Soon the male tourists in our group were herded into two small rooms to view the famous pornographic frescoes. One, B. told me afterward, showed an old man with a tremendous phallus, one a lewd variation of the sexual act. During this cultural tour, the ladies were shoved into the kitchen, since Italian law forbids all but adult men to inspect the off-color art. As the gentlemen filed out, looking sheepish, a child ran in alarm to his father, crying,

"Papa, Papa, what were you *doing* in there?" He turned to his
wife and groaned.

All the while Vesuvius gazed down, measuring our pride,
our vulnerability, and we shivered and moved on. At the public
baths the pitiful forms of two slaves were caught in a moment
of choking death. I noted what agony is and turned away
(far from agreeing with Emily Dickinson's foolish words, "I
like the look of agony, / Because I know it's true").

The walk took us through streets furrowed by chariot
wheels. Our footsteps matched their footsteps—the lost, betrayed Pompeïans. At the final spectacle, a snack bar with the
sign "*Bevete Coca-Cola*," the circle was complete, we were
here. Yet how is mortal catastrophe ever stopped? It only
begins over again, and a world stands still.

Past the rocky island of Ithaca, the *Vulcania* entered the
Gulf of Corinth, gliding between mountains with the Pelopon-
nesus on one side, the Greek mainland on the other. I sat
drinking tea in the lounge, listening to the ship's orchestra.

Within an hour we would reach Patras, end of our present
journey. Uneasily I found myself reliving a moment a few
years ago when I had sat drinking tea in the Adelphi Hotel,
Liverpool, waiting with B. to sail at midnight across the Irish
Sea to Dublin. Without warning I had become homesick,
faint, physically sick with a longing for home. It was horrible.
Clutching my teacup that winter afternoon, I listened to the
hotel orchestra playing a tinkling popular tune, "The Third
Man." I shut my eyes. I thought I would die.

At that instant today, the same nausea and panic rose in
my throat. I stared at the empty Greek sea. "Dear God, it's
happening again!" The teacup shook in my hand and I closed
my eyes. As if on signal, the ship's orchestra launched briskly
into the next number—"The Third Man." I think I must be
psychic.

The local bus from Athens to Eleusis had a lighted holy
picture of the Virgin above two artificial birds and a vase of
purple anemones. A Greek girl wore a head scarf labeled
"Souvenir of Atlantic City." We rattled the twelve miles out

of Athens along the Sacred Way lined with olive trees—once lined centuries before Christ with stately tombs, monuments, marble temples that the pilgrims passed. They walked instead of taking a bus. Or they danced along and sang.

Eleusis is a small village now, known for its soap works. Opposite lies Salamis, where in 480 B.C. Themistocles rammed and sank the ships of the Persians, while Xerxes watched on shore seated elegantly on a golden throne under a gold umbrella. Four or five ships moved in the blue harbor today.

Inside the great square hall of the Mystery of Mysteries (or the rubble left of it), we stood utterly alone. The sacred enclosure, once surrounded by a high fortified wall, was meant to keep out people like us. To enter was forbidden the uninitiated on pain of death. Yet here we stood, unpunished, guilty of neglect of the gods, undevout among the scattered ruins—where tiers of rock-cut seats had risen up to contain three thousand. Here the mysteries of life and death had been revealed. Here was the final act of Beholding in blinding flashes of torchlight.

What really happened during the thousand years of the Eleusinian mysteries no one has ever told. The secrets (that I wish I knew) were well kept. To unfold them was not only punishable by death but, far worse, punishable for eternity by the gods themselves. The Homeric hymn to Demeter says:

Happy is he among the inhabitants of the earth who has contemplated these great spectacles. But he who is not initiated is forever deprived of such happiness even when death has brought him down to the dark dwelling place.

But then Theodosius came to Greece from Byzantium and, in the name of Christianity, destroyed Eleusis.

Whatever the revelations were, they gave boundless joy to the beholders, relieved them of guilt and placed them under the particular care of the gods, who loved and forgave. At Eleusis (meaning "the arrival"), the pilgrims arrived at the ultimate truth. They learned the answers: why we came and where we are going. If they suffered momentary terror at a glimpse of hell, this gave way to the sublime vision of bliss and the Elysian fields.

(Lucian said the Elysian fields were near the moon—the
Isles of the Blessed. "The fields there bring forth loaves of
readymade bread. There are 365 fountains of honey and 500
of sweet-scented oil, 7 rivers of milk and 8 of wine. The large
trees are made of the finest glass and the fruit of them are cups
which fill with wine." Unlike Eden, no fruit on those trees
was forbidden.)

Even to children and slaves was paradise made visible, even
to prostitutes. Only murderers were shut out; only the uninitiated like us were deprived of the certainty, the final serene
joy of knowing. It was too late to solve the mystery now.

"I should like a stone from Greece," writes Peggy, "a small
stone, from the sea or from the Acropolis if Lord Elgin left
any behind. David objects to my asking. He would have me
do away with sentimental attachments to stones." I've been
intending anyway to pick up a pebble or two, lawless though
it is in Greece. I once had a fine stone collection that Lizzie
threw out. A boulder came from Watkins Glen, N.Y., a rock
from Niagara Falls; I cherished them over seashells or paper
dolls. Lizzie saved everything but my stones.

I kneel down and search in the rubble at Eleusis.

Today two American friends, Sigmund and Lys, took us in
their new Porsche to Marathon. We rode in squeezed elegance
in the tiny two-seater sports car with a bottle of ouzo squeezed
in beside us. The ride across the mountain was so spectacular
that when I yelled "Sigmund!" he thought I was overcome by
magnificence and agreed. "Isn't it incredible?"

I was overcome by the breakneck speed with which we
rounded curves and dashed beside precipices, with no fence
to stop us from diving down the side. As Sigmund drove with
one hand, he looked past his shoulder making ecstatic gestures.
The car raced on unguided. We rode in swank to certain
destruction.

At the highest peak, Sigmund drew over to the edge of the
precipice and stopped. Lys's knuckles were white as she
gripped the seat. I closed my eyes, sure in the furious wind the
little car would blow off the cliff and plunge us into the Aegean

Sea a mile below. When I opened them cautiously, we were gazing on Marathon.

> The mountains look on Marathon—
> And Marathon looks on the sea.

Mt. Pentelicus was our marble mountain, from which the Pentelic marble was quarried and taken along this road on wooden sleds for the building of the Parthenon. From this mountain a beacon flame told Athens the Persians had landed at Marathon. Down we sped, following the steep winding path recently made passable for Porsches, down the ancient road to the plain.

Marathon, six miles of it, a marshy strip between mountains and sea, lay crowned with olive trees. We jumped from the car, ran to the battlefield, and scaled another height. A narrow flight of 56 steps led to the grassy top of the Tumulus, a forty-foot tomb of the Athenian footsoldiers who halted the Persians near this mound on August 12, 480 B.C. A mere 192 Athenians died that day, while the turbaned Persians fleeing in panic to their ships lost six thousand. The battle took less than three hours. Aeschylus fought; his brother died when his hands were cut off by the Persians. The victor was Miltiades, who saved all Greece by his blazing courage.

I looked about me, thinking "Here Byron stood!" He stood at Marathon in 1810, on a sightseeing tour with his friend Hobhouse, a pompous ass with whom (Byron complained) he wrangled every moment of the tour. Yet amid tiffs, squabbles, and bawling out Hobhouse, he found time to muse an hour alone—the poem says—dreaming that Greece might still be free. Byron claimed the Greeks tried to sell him Marathon, offering it for £900, though the poem never said he wanted to *buy* the place.

"Here every night," wrote Pausanias, "you may hear the horses neighing and the men fighting." You need keen ears, since no horses were used in the battle. In the Greek sunshine, dreaming the hour away like Byron, we heard no sound at all.

The ouzo had set us free, at least carefree. Christopher Rand, writing about Greece, said he met an American in a bar in

Athens who objected to drinking ouzo. "It goes to the head," he said, ordering a double Scotch.

Plato walked beside us in the Agora and Socrates talked. (Fielding said Socrates had the face of a rogue, though those who knew him saw the likeness to Silenus, son of Pan, the fat, drunken companion of Bacchus). But here he walked and here he died by order of the tribunal who judged him guilty of denying the gods. And here centuries later St. Paul walked alone, speaking sternly, "You men of Athens, I perceive that in all things you are too superstitious."

Flying by Olympic Airlines to Crete, fifty minutes from Athens over the Aegean, I hoped not to fall into the sea like Icarus. Let me be Daedalus instead, "old father, old artificer," soaring at 10,000 feet on steady wings to safety and long life.

Ulysses says in the *Odyssey:* "Amidst the wine-dark sea lies Crete, a fair rich island populous beyond compute, with ninety cities."

Mr. Theodore Karusses revealed it to us, a wise Cretan about sixty years old, gray-haired with dark somber eyes. He had been foreman of excavations at Knossos, now served as guide to Crete. Through him I learned what the books couldn't convey. I saw a little of the Minoan world, where Greece had her birth.

On the first day, Mr. Karusses took us by car from Heraklion over the lonely mountain roads to Phaestos, forty miles distant. Five of us rode in the battered old Pontiac, including the driver who spoke no English and a young man from Connecticut whom I had seen at lunch yesterday in Athens. "Was I so conspicuous?" Mr. Barnard asked surprised. In Greece he was.

On the outskirts of Heraklion, Mr. Karusses pointed to three mountain peaks, the three homes of Zeus. On Mt. Dicte Zeus was born (and his umbilical cord fell beside the river Triton), on Mt. Ida he was reared in a cave, on Mt. Louktas he died and was buried. Thus the saying goes that the people of Crete are liars, of such proportions they killed off and buried the immortal Zeus. Cretans are liars, goes another saying, but since a Cretan said so it is obviously a lie.

Spring flowered in February—the yellow oxalis spread over the fields like sunshine. Marguerites, anemones, red poppies bloomed by the roadside. In Crete are 7 cities (not the 90 of Homer) and 1,540 villages, Mr. Karusses recited like a patient schoolmaster.

The small white rocks on the hills were sheep, the black rocks goats. No farmhouse stood near, for Cretans and Greeks alike choose to live together in villages and go out each day on a donkey to work the land. "People never steal in the villages," said Mr. Karusses. "They kill, yes, but they do not steal."

The road became a mud hole, all but impassable. I sat beside the driver, who steered with one hand, blowing his horn with the other on an empty road beside a precipice. Mr. Karusses talked in a calm flowing stream as if we were in a museum. Soon he got to Minoan culture.

"They worshipped gods in the form of nature—the bird, the snake, the bull," he said, "whereas in Greece they worshipped gods in the form of the human body. From the start woman was worshipped as a deity in Crete."

"She had a body," I said.

He smiled. "As a source of life she represented nature. Like the earth she was fertile, the Mother, made fertile by the male god incarnate in the bull."

I didn't say so, but that bull myth upsets me. Somewhere along the line it got out of hand and reversed itself. When Zeus as a white bull seduced the girl Europa (right here in Crete under a' plane tree), he wasn't a male god serving the Goddess. He was *the* God.

From this union was born a son, King Minos, for whose royal sake the god Poseidon caused a sacred white bull to emerge from the sea. Pasiphae, the wife of Minos, having conceived a violent passion for Poseidon's bull, ordered Daedalus to construct a heifer out of wood. This he fashioned so cunningly that, with Pasiphae concealed inside, the bull was thoroughly deceived. From *this* union ("the proof of lust unspeakable," said Virgil, "the infamy of Crete," said Dante) came the fearful Minotaur (or Minos bull), a man with a bull's head whom King Minos hid in shame in the labyrinth at Knossos. There the monster that fed only on human flesh devoured seven Athenian youths and seven maidens each year till Theseus came from Athens and killed him off. My soul, what a bull story!

"Nothing in the world is new," Mr. Karusses was saying with a faroff look. "It has all happened before."

Descending among pomegranate trees and yellow marguerites, we drove on the plain beneath snowcapped Mt. Ida. The weather was sunny and hot. "The donkey freezes in the morning from the cold. He stinks in the afternoon from the heat." Mr. Karusses again.

The Palace of Phaestos stood unfortified on the level summit of a rocky hill. On foot we climbed up a steep pitch to the massive ruins, alone in the forsaken place. Mr. Karusses, puffing, made a joke: "You see, we have no need to gaze at ruins. After such a climb we are ruined already." The stately palace rose, what remained of it, above a spectacular setting of gold fields of oxalis on the Mesara plain. Mt. Ida lifted crowns of snow, beyond lay the sea. "Nature helps," said Mr. Karusses, and a lizard darted under a rock.

Phaestos, unlike Knossos, has never been restored. A few archaeologists believe in restoration; most of them object. Mr. Karusses gave the "professors' view": fifty percent of restoration at most is accurate, twenty-five percent doubtful; for the rest it's human to make mistakes. He relished this bit of wisdom and said it twice, offering a further item for solemn thought—the preservation of ruins is the means of destroying them. Phaestos lay safely buried for four thousand years, its history intact in the earth. Brought by modern excavation into existence, it has deteriorated in the fifty years of its new life more than in the whole period of its burial. Each step taken (each step we took) helps to crumble the stones. So men bring the past to life to destroy it. What palaces are waiting, intact, hidden still?

A mass of rubble lay before our eyes. The three upper storeys had disappeared; only the terraces, the sweeping staircase, the stone bull's horns were left. The Minoan kings reigned while the Pharaohs ruled in Egypt. Homer spoke of Phaestos;

King Minos may have built it. Here it rose in magnificence and here it fell. I like the legend "Its inhabitants were famous for their wit," though the palace keeps no echo of them now. "Listen, we hear nothing," said Mr. Karusses.

Returning by the same route over the mountains ("the purgatory road," Mr. Barnard called it), despite the driver's maneuvering we slued and were stuck deep in mud. The men climbed out in a foot of water to rock the car back and forth to set it free. "God damn!" said the driver who knew no English.

B. glanced over the precipice inches away, with no guardrail. "It's straight down," he said.

"They say you go quickly," observed Mr. Barnard.

Next day Mr. Karusses took us (without Mr. Barnard whose nerves were shattered) in the old car to Knossos, five miles from Heraklion. More splendid than Phaestos, it consisted of ten acres of a fabulous palace of 1600 rooms. We were alone in a high wind, speechless at the Minoan wonder of the world, once five storeys of it with grand staircases, royal apartments, corridors of 22 storerooms that kept wine jars tall as a man, four gates leading to the four points of the compass. It gave me a feeling of unutterable riches.

It gave me a feeling too of panic. As Mr. Karusses led us through the winding labyrinth of rooms—the infamous Labyrinth from which few found their way out—I felt lost, trapped, never to be seen again. How could Mr. Karusses bring us back alive? Even Theseus had followed a skein of thread with the help of Ariadne, King Minos' daughter.

Some joker said this is not Crete but concrete. Yet the partial restoration with its warmth of sunbaked orange brick brought renewed life to the palace, a sense of happy people— the lovely slim women, bejewelled, white-skinned, with black curls, bare breasts; the handsome ruddy men—living in a riot of blues and reds splashed on pavement, ceilings, walls. It excited an imagination as ignorant as mine. I was glad to be shown something even fifty percent right. Knossos was sacked and destroyed about 1400 B.C. Why were no skeletons found? At least half the Minoans must have got lost in that labyrinth.

Out in the courtyard Mr. Karusses stooped to pick up a piece of yellow pottery, a painted shard from an earthen pot. This he offered me with a bow, and I gasped to receive it. Two painted heavy black lines were once part of a pattern in a Minoan mind.

Late that afternoon our guide dropped us at our hotel, his shoulders sagging, his words gone. We had spent two days together: a lovable man, informed, patient, thorough. We had listened, he knew that. He turned and warmly clasped our hands. In a low voice B. spoke of his fee.

"The matter is arranged at the tour office," he answered. "I have no authority. I'm just the guide."

"You are the teacher," I said. Mr. Karusses smiled and slowly nodded his head.

The Greek women Aphrodite and Marika telephoned, "We have party, please. You come tonight?" We went to their flat in Kifissia, a suburb of Athens. Only Janine was there as guest, and the maid Angela part of the family. Their English is pidgin but plentiful. It was carnival time, Ash Monday, end of rejoicing before Lent.

Aphrodite, till recently an opera singer in Athens, now in her forties, plump and pretty, decked herself in a heavy pink satin kimono, blossoms in her beehive hairdo, eyes painted into Japanese slits. She sang the aria of Butterfly's grief with modesty, passion, and not much voice. Stout Marika, like Aphrodite unmarried, put on carnival costume, a black-and-white striped sailor suit with red ribbons in her pigtails. Janine wore a black domino. B. and I came as ourselves.

We laughed because it was hilarious—Marika twisting her braids and picking up her heels. We danced, in Greece where one rises and dances solo, stamping and swirling to the music. We danced in turn and together, crying "Bravo, bravo!" at each performance.

Tomorrow we cry, tonight we laugh—Marika's view. "I shed big tears at breakfast." When their father was imprisoned during the German Occupation, the sisters weak from hunger walked back and forth the ten miles to Athens to carry him bits of food from their starvation hoard. Now they are plump and alone. Twenty-five years ago Aphrodite's lover married another girl since she had no dowry to bring him; yet he visits her daily, still her lover. His daughter Janine avoids her mother and spends weekends with Aphrodite, whom she worships. Aphrodite is meant for love.

Angela with the goddess-beautiful face, will she too cry tomorrow? She stood in the doorway doubled up with laughter. Once she gave Aphrodite a playful slap on her behind.

M A R C H .   We had a three-day blizzard in Istanbul. B. and I had sailed to Byzantium (Constantinople, Istanbul, Stamboul, take your choice) with visions in our heads. We came from Athens over the Aegean on the *San Marco*, a miniature Italian ship of great charm. Its stewards were haughty, its menus in Italian and French, the movie in German, currency in liras, drachmas, dollars, Turkish pounds, and there was no soap. It was like sailing with the international set. Among the Cyclades on a blue sea, we scanned the newspapers that told of heavy snows in Europe. An article in the London *Times* lamented the plight of the bearded tit—what would be its fate?

I was happy to sail the seas like Yeats (who never went) and by way of the Aegean, Dardanelles, Sea of Marmara, come "to the holy city of Byzantium." At the mouth of the Bosphorus, mosques and minarets of the old city glowed, the dome of St. Sophia glittered gold in the sunlight.

For a few sunny days we wandered about fabulous Istanbul, a city astride two continents. We crossed the Atatürk Bridge to walk in old Byzantium. High walls once surrounded it. The body of a Byzantine emperor was found at the main gate where he fought the last siege. Five hundred years ago its Byzantine churches were turned into Turkish mosques, the images of Christ and Mary plastered over and forgotten for centuries. In the Blue Mosque of Sultan Ahmed, blue was the color of Mohammed's paradise.

Then the snow fell.

Emerging from dinner at the Istanbul-Hilton, wellfed and

overcharged, we found a blanketed city, our taxi a white igloo. The driver cut through slippery streets in a veil of snow, raced hellbent down a cobbled alley, and turned the corner to our hotel, the Pera Palace. With an outcry he slammed on the brakes and stopped short. We pitched from our seats to the floor. Two or three bodies hurtled against the car, rocking it nearly off its wheels. We had arrived in the middle of a furious street fight, surrounded by a dozen angry Turks who threw each other to the ground, falling about us as if we were a prize they fought and died for. The driver, leaping out, pulled me from the cab into the midst of it. A man fell with a groan at my feet, bleeding in the snow. I stood paralyzed before him. He seemed badly hurt.

"Hurry, lady!" the driver whispered. Shielding me with both arms, he dodged through the fighters into the hotel, B. close behind. After receiving his money, the driver rushed out panting, battled his way to his taxi, started it and backed away.

At the bay window of the Pera Palace, we watched with horror the brutal fight, the bloody man lying unconscious in the street. The hotel clerk shrugged and returned to his desk. "It's the snow," he said. "Turks have bad tempers. Snow in March makes us angry."

I thought of Hilaire Belloc's line, "I have the temper of a Turk," but it didn't sound funny. I said, "Please call the police. That man may be dying." The clerk shrugged.

Finally they gave up, shaking their fists. Two fighters dragged the wounded man to a car across the street. The others disappeared. Bright red blood stained the pavement, and the covering snow fell.

Next morning we woke to a blizzard, the snow horizontal in fierce gusts. Byzantium was blotted out. In the street below, the horns of stalled cars sounded like angry Turkish geese. We thought of places to visit—Byzantium's 500 mosques, Scutari across the river in Asia Minor, up the Bosphorus to the Black Sea. Not a chance. We would leave this wretched Istanbul, not by air since all planes were grounded, not by sea back to the isles of Greece, but north to Europe by the best exit left. Surely the trains still ran—the European glamor expresses, the *trains-de-luxe* of romance and intrigue, to Paris, Vienna, London. The Orient Express! The Balkan Express! That was it, back to civilization out of this dreary hole, Byzantium.

For the next three days while the snow fell, we tried and failed. Two large Communist countries stood between us and freedom; we spent our time humbly requesting transit visas, going to sit patient in the Bulgarian and Yugoslavian consulates. We waded through snowdrifts, climbed pitchdark stairs, waited like refugees in unlit rooms, since there was no electricity. We learned that the Bulgarians and Yugoslavs, like the Turks, were angry. They scowled, ignored us, took away our passports ordering us to wait 24 hours before returning; anyway we must have photographs. But the photographers had shut up shop and gone home to wait out the big snow.

At last we stumbled up some stairs to the bleak rooms of S. Blum, a Romanian Jew who lived with two canaries and wasn't angry. In French he urged us into his abode where with no light he went ahead and took our pictures, which turned out unimaginably grim. "*Très joli, Madame*," he cried in ecstasy. "*Oh la, c'est gentil, très joli!*" In a crisis my French leaves me, and all I can remember is the Marseillaise. "*Allons*," I said. "*Marchons, marchons.*"

By the third morning we were all but routed. So far we had gained grudging permission to cross Yugoslavia, and it was Saturday. B. set out alone to beg or bribe the Bulgarians into granting us a visa and to retrieve our passports. "With my shield or on it, I return," he said. If the Bulgarian consulate wasn't closed for the weekend, if by now they were sick of our faces, we might depart at noon on the Balkan Express for Vienna. Or, more likely, we might not.

At 11:30, B. burst into our room flushed, victorious. Packed and ready, holding my worry beads (as I had seen old men carrying them in Turkey), I stood gazing at a city obliterated, lost, a world of angry Turks, street brawls, snow. And still it snowed.

"Anyway, I'm glad we've come."

"To the holy city of Byzantium?" asked B. laughing.

Worry beads were brought to Greece by the Turks during the Occupation. You see men from Athens to Istanbul walking on the street gripping their string of beads or sitting in a café telling them like a rosary. I don't know what the women do to lighten their worries. The finest beads are amber, and I've heard the number is important, as many as 33, 66, or 99 to a string. Nowadays they come sometimes large as marbles or hen's eggs, the world being what it is. The Greeks say they have no religious significance; they occupy the hands, soothe the nerves (some call them "nervous" beads or "patience" beads), and guard against anxiety, disquiet, and care.

My worry beads from Athens—a cheap string of fifteen beads with a yellow tassel—are pitiful to look at, but they serve the purpose. Each bead offers solace, or is meant to:

First bead:	"Nothing that is so is so."
Second bead:	"My desolation does begin to make a better life."
Third bead:	"The devyll, they say, is dede, The devyll is dede."
Fourth bead:	"Whatever tears one may shed, in the end one always blows one's nose."
Fifth bead:	"He'd crack his wits Day after day, yet never find the meaning. *And then he laughed to think that what seemed hard Should be so simple—*"
Sixth bead:	"Nobody loses all the time."
Seventh bead:	When Simonides offered to teach Themistocles the art of memory, he answered, "Ah, rather teach me the art of forgetting; for I often remember what I would not, and cannot forget what I would."
Eighth bead:	"We are all frail. . . . Nay, women are frail too."
Ninth bead:	"I hold a mouses herte nat worth a leek That hath but oon hole for to sterte to."
Tenth bead:	"The world is but a cherry fair."
Eleventh bead:	"Man, please thy maker, and be merry, And give not of this world a cherry."
Twelfth bead:	"In every country, dogges bite."
Thirteenth bead:	"Only to gods in heaven Comes no old age, nor death of anything; All else is turmoiled by our master Time."

Fourteenth bead: "Be you not troubled with the time which
                     drives
                     O'er your content these strong necessities."
Fifteenth bead: "All is eterne in mutabilitie."

I'm sorry I failed to buy a tear bottle in Istanbul, the better
to hold my tears. When I saw them, I didn't know what they
were for—small, narrow-necked bottles of terracotta or glass
shaped like a bulb or flask. Such vessels were found in Roman
and late Greek tombs, used by the mourners to drop their
tears into, too small to hold a copious flood.

And the Psalmist addressed God, "Thou tellest my wander-
ings: put thou my tears into thy bottle: are they not in thy
book?"

The Balkan Express. The Sirkeci railroad terminal at Istanbul was noisy, crowded with shawled and kerchiefed women,
men carrying packs on their backs, in their hands a string of
worry beads. A Bulgarian woman, a green shawl over her head
and the corners held in her teeth, lugged a basket with a
pair of Turkish slippers sticking out the end. B. and I with
six pieces of luggage on a truck looked out of place, like
Americans traveling first class. Our Turkish porter made signs
it was traintime. At 1:00 P.M. Saturday the Balkan Express
drew in, bound for Sofia, Belgrade, and Vienna.

Ten minutes earlier, it had occurred to me to take some food
along on a forty-hour journey to Vienna. Knowing no Turkish,
I hadn't succeeded in buying much. When I said "oranges" in
the station restaurant, the waiter brought a cup of coffee. He
offered honey desserts and milk puddings, then conducted me
to the kitchen to inspect the stewed lamb. I shook my head.
"Bread! Meat!" I cried, pretending to eat a sandwich. He
rolled his eyes. By running about and pointing, I got two
oranges, two rolls, a piece of cold chicken. The idea of bottled
water seemed too fanciful to act out.

Only one small *wagon-lit* was attached like a caboose to the
rear of the train. It took two porters and the conductor to
squeeze us into our compartment, with the lunch, our winter
coats, overshoes, six pieces of luggage including a typewriter

and small trunk. The sink when closed served as a table but left no room for my feet, on which I sat. We barely managed a deep breath. Yet we gazed thankfully out the dirty window at the Golden Horn. A ship moved and a seagull flew overhead. It still snowed.

An hour passed but the train didn't start. It was packed to bursting except in our *wagon-lit,* where the other six passengers talked in Turkish and German. Then a shrill female voice in Turkish came over a loudspeaker, and a group on the station platform stood transfixed. They gestured their alarm. Somebody wailed. As minutes passed, people fled the train in large numbers, hurrying down the platform with their babies and belongings.

The conductor put his head into our compartment. He knew a word or two of English, which came to him fitfully. "Big snow," he said, pointing up the track. We nodded. He thought a while and found two more words: "Eight o'clock," pointing to the clock outside the window. "Maybe go," he added with a sigh, "maybe not," and collecting our passports locked the outside doors of the sleeping car. We decided to stay put.

By 5:00 P.M. it was dark and cold, with little heat from a woodburning stove. Nobody in our car had left the train. Nobody raised his voice in complaint or dismay. The talk around us was animated. No spies, no sirens, no criminal types in dark glasses appeared to be aboard. Two old women in the corridor, one Turkish, one perhaps Austrian, were becoming fast friends in voluble German. The conductor offered to go out and buy for us two bottles of beer. On his return he bowed at the tip with a sociable smile.

At 7:00 P.M. we opened our package of lunch and had supper by the light of the station platform. It was a picnic in a clothes closet. To save the battery, no lights were permitted till the train started. We ate all our food, feeling mellow and resigned, better off here than marooned in heavy snows in the mountains. No doubt they were clearing the tracks up ahead.

The conductor came bearing sensational news: "We go." Exactly eight o'clock. From an empty platform the Balkan Express moved toward the outskirts of Istanbul and frontiers of Bulgaria. Through a curtain of snow, we glimpsed a child waving from a lighted window, a father pouring wine at his table.

In the countryside the snow grew deeper, piled in alps along the tracks. Ice formed on the windows. The train struggled hard, pausing, starting with a grinding of wheels, straining through the storm. In the dim light I read a guidebook to Vienna, baffled by the baroque splendors. One fact emerged: the blue Danube isn't blue. When our berths were made up, piled with luggage, I slept in my clothes my arm around a suitcase.

Sunday morning. In what seemed Siberia, we surveyed a white wilderness. Lord only knew where we were. Out in the corridor with the six other passengers, I timidly asked the Austrian lady, *"Bitte, ist das Bulgaria?"* and she laughed, answering in English, "Not likely! No, it's Turkey!" We had stood still most of the night in the snows of Turkey.

What a charming woman she was, the Viennese lady, full of gaiety, vivacity, wit. But she was old—at perhaps sixty—with a worn lined face and eyes washed as by tears. In halting English she said a word about herself. "I take journeys, you see, like this—" She bit her lip. "It no longer matters what I do. I lost all, all, all in the war, my husband, my three sons. So I take journeys. Like this—"

She was returning from Iraq, where the street fighting in Baghdad had not deterred her. "No one bothers an old woman. I cannot change the world. I cannot stop the hate. I go to Greece, Persia, and this I enjoy. In life is nothing left. But this I enjoy."

No restaurant car had been attached to the train. B. and I wondered where our next meal was coming from. By noon we reached the frontier of Bulgaria where two customs officials entered our compartment and made a thorough search for contraband in the water cabinet. It contained a carafe and one paper towel.

During the two-hour wait at the border, I sat cramped in my seat listening to the chatter of the Viennese and the Turkish lady as they ran back and forth in bedroom slippers, sharing a banana, giggling. They had plenty of stamina, plenty of style.

When the train moved, the Viennese looked in the door and winked, making a face at the country we were allowed to enter. "They are slaves," she said.

The sun beat down, the snow blinded. In a muddy Bulgarian village two squealing pigs were tied on the common, guarded by a Communist soldier. In the city of Plovdiv, I studied a statue in the square.

"Stalin or Khrushchev?" a young Turk asked, standing beside me.

"Too thin. Must be Lenin."

B. had spotted the station restaurant and tried to get off the train. The conductor barred the way, spitting in anger. "They will sell you nothing," said the young Turk. "You must pay in leva, Bulgarian money." It was late afternoon, we were hungry. "This is not free peoples," he went on. "They are afraid to breathe. Turkey is different, it is free, a republic. You saw that?"

At Sofia a station guard stood watch to prevent anyone from leaving the train. But our carafe was empty; we were in dire need of drinking water. I snatched up the carafe, jumped off the train, and dodged across to the room marked "Dames" before he could stop me. A peasant woman drew me water from the tap, and I raced back in time to see the train move away. With a frantic spurt I ran and hurled myself aboard.

"They left me behind!" I cried to B. "What were you going to do?"

"Stop the train."

But I was frightened. I had lost faith in the Balkan Express to give a damn what happened to me.

At the frontier of Yugoslavia, a frowning official confiscated my typewriter, locked in its case in the luggage rack. "Capitalists!" he muttered. I felt guilty of espionage. At the end of the three-hour wait, he returned redfaced with the typewriter and two declaration forms that in a fury he ordered me to fill out.

By nightfall, more than 24 hours after leaving Istanbul on what we had assumed to be one of the fastest crack expresses in Europe (where an attendant would say, *Messieurs les voyageurs, le dîner est servi!*" and the passengers danced and drank Veuve Cliquot), we were starved. The new conductor told us curtly there would be nothing to eat till we reached Vienna, another night and day away. *"Pas de manger,"* he said without regret. In bed B. studied the list of restaurants in England's *Blue Guide,* and in the mountains of Yugoslavia I dreamed of Greece, its roast lamb and civilized people.

Monday. I lay in the upper berth, thinking of Agatha Christie. In her novel twelve passengers en route to Europe boarded the Orient Express in Istanbul in 1935, feasted on champagne and oysters; and the murder occurred about here, in the same snows of Yugoslavia. At noon we reached Zagreb, where the word *Tito* with a red star covered the whole side of a building. Again the countryside became white haystacks, white vineyards, a frozen stream. The Viennese lady said a ten-year-old Persian boy in third class had been left behind in Zagreb when the train started up with no warning. What would a terrified child do without language, money, passport?

I felt dirty and, like the train, I was. Yet no one grew querulous at discomforts. They were seasoned travelers on the Balkan Express, who knew what not to expect: food, water, clean toilets, warmth, information, the amenities or the necessities. On a train already a day late, nobody asked questions. Endurance would get us there in the end.

By afternoon the Yugoslav scenery grew stupendous with mountain peaks and bulbous onion-spired churches perched near the gods. The Turkish lady offered me a cigarette (please, lady, just a banana?). I begged the Viennese to tell me about the sights in store in Vienna.

"Soon, dear child, soon. We will sit and have our little chat. But now, no, impossible. The view is too *schön* for words."

She was a real traveler, who had come for the ride. To her it was better to travel than to arrive. To her the journey was everything.

As we approached the Austrian frontier, "The time has come," she said. Side by side in her compartment, we opened my guidebook to Vienna, and her eyes shone as she leafed through the pages. "My city!" One visits the State Opera, of course, the Hapsburg Palace, the Vienna woods. One admires the baroque ("I do not like it. I prefer simple things"), one eats the Sachertorte ("I do not like it, but one eats it"). I asked if one also stays at the Sacher Hotel, where the famous chocolate cake is made. She glared at me horrified.

"But you are mad! You are *mad!* It is not for you and me. It is for archdukes and emperors!" She quickly apologized. "Pardon my rudeness, I am stupid. I do not know if you are so rich."

The late proprietor, Anna Sacher, was a woman who served emperors and kings, treating them "exactly as you treat your husband." I wondered what she meant by that.

I had underlined a description of Hitler shouting from the balcony of the Hofburg Palace to announce the occupation of Austria. Later the portraits of Lenin and Stalin hung from the same imperial façade. The Viennese lady shut the book, her eyes filled with tears. "No, no, no, I *beg* you, implore you! Love my country. These terrible times are past. We must live, we must forget."

Late on Monday afternoon we entered Austria. At Spielfeld-Strasse, our *wagon-lit* was joined to the Austrian Express and became a *Schlafwagen.* Outside the Balkans we were free. We had changed worlds, and the train rushed along, free itself, carrying, could it be, *sandwiches!* B. and I devoured two ham sandwiches apiece, stuffing them in our mouths, the first food since Istanbul two days ago, a journey of a hundred years.

At sunset we entered an enchanted Austrian valley, where a pink sky repeated itself in the river. By moonlight we were high in the peaks, a floodlit *Schloss* stood out like an amusement park, and we descended, dropping to where the lights of villages greeted us below.

At midnight we drew into the modern terminal at Vienna, twenty hours late, and what had we seen?—a world of snow, a wintry Bulgaria, a white Yugoslavia barren as the moon. But in our minds it had been a farther journey, across a frontier to another world. There was no doubt which choice of worlds we made.

"One thing I pray you, love my country," said the Viennese lady in farewell. She hadn't asked my name nor I hers. We wouldn't meet again. "I wish you a good journey in this life, my friend," she said. "Most of all, I wish you peace. *Auf Wiedersehen.*"

A banquet in Vienna: we took Vienna mouthful by mouthful (somebody said it smells like caraway seeds). Everything about it looked ample and wellfed—the pretty women in the street, the fleshy baroque statues, the broad Lippizaner stallions, the massive public monuments. Maria Theresa was a decidedly stout empress.

The Viennese eat five meals a day, and so did we. After a heavy breakfast we went in sunshine and slush for hot chocolate *mit Schlag* at the Café Mozart and read the New York *Times.* Then it was time for lunch. The rotund waiter at the Hofburg Restaurant near the Palace served us Wienerschnitzel, mit Bier, purring softly as he went. Like the fat, butter-yellow cat at my feet, *"Bitte schön,"* he purred. *"Bitte sehr."*

We listened to Strauss waltzes and ate in waltz-time. After lunch I began to feel hungry. Strolling on the Ringstrasse, we stopped at a luxury grocery store, Julius Meinl's, to gaze fondly at the foreign specialties on display—Richelieu canned peaches from Chicago.

For afternoon tea at the Sacher Hotel, we tried the Sachertorte under glittering crystal chandeliers with waiters like grand dukes. It was fare worthy of the portliest Hapsburg, a rich dark chocolate cake with inch-high chocolate icing smothered in whipped cream.

I could hardly wait for dinner. Hurrying to *Zur Linde,* a 500-year-old restaurant near St. Stephen's Cathedral (whose slender spire was the one thin sight all day), we asked ourselves what Brahms would have had tonight. This was his favorite eating place. After delicate thought we chose the Bauernschmaus, a large symphony of dumplings, sauerkraut, pickles, roast pork, pork tenderloin, and sausages. Mit Wein, ja, ja. For dessert there was "scrumbled pancake mit mush of plums."

At the performance of *Don Giovanni* that night at the Vienna State Opera, the coloratura looked plump as a fat pigeon, delectable, so sharpening to the appetite we felt the need of a little supper afterward. In a beer cellar, the Löwenbräukeller, B. inquired what a particular item on the menu was, and the buxom waitress put her hands to her head to make two pointed horns.

"Goat," we said, but ordered it anyway.

The waitress brought a smoking platter of meat, which we regarded with pleasure but perplexity. Glad to enlighten us, she yelled over to the counter man to supply the English word. He scratched his head till it came to him.

"Deer," he said. And so it was, venison.

Cambridge. The Royal Hotel on Trumpington Street is done in early Biedermeier, with bulging carved furniture of yellow oak, Chinese vases and other chinoiserie, hideous statuary, ormolu clocks that don't run, artificial flowers—not like the Pera Palace in Istanbul reminiscent of a more florid and palatial time. This inglorious stuff collected from junk shops and auctions was always secondhand.

Queen Elizabeth I is framed full-length on the landing. We have a shabby room on the ground floor overlooking a piece of garden and a pile of coal. The maid says, "Ow, you're in the bridal suite," though with a double bed, a twin bed, and a single cot I don't know what kind of honeymoon is expected. I work beside the dilapidated gas fire, while B. goes to the University library which rises like a railway terminal behind Clare College. For a noon walk to meet him, I pass Peterhouse and Pembroke ("My mother Cambridge," wrote Spenser at Pembroke), or wander into the quads of Corpus Christi and King's, where the students emerge on bicycles like bats out of hell, their black gowns streaming in the wind. On the bulletin boards is the usual thing: "Notice of training for boat races: one pint of beer a day maximum." "The May Ball will be held on June 10."

The English are undeviating. The pattern is eccentric but monotonous, with Cambridge keeping to her ancient ways and streets too narrow for the snarled traffic. When I feel exasperated, I walk along the Cam under the green willows and forgive everybody. A fat white swan waddles on the bank, wild ducks fly over my nose, circle, and return to skim the water like a plane. This is Cambridge of the Crocuses. They spring up along the backs, interwoven like a Persian carpet, white, purple, saffron, lavender, gold.

At Woolworth's the up escalator carries a sign, "No downward thoroughfare." The sale is brisk of Mother's Day (Mothering Sunday) cards—"To Our Mum," "Larks, dear Mummy." A mother and child stand before a display of sponges. "I don't suppose you remember having a *real* sponge, darling," she says wistfully. "You're so used to the horrid plastic ones."

An aged lady and her spiteful hired companion are fixtures in the Royal Hotel lounge. The old lady is senile and infirm, helpless to issue commands, bullied, cringing, despised, stuck here in misery till she dies. "But she is very rich!" says the parlor maid. "Very, very rich."

At teatime I read the *Cambridge News:* an article on "The British Housewife's Strange Attitude towards Vegetables"; an advertisement recommending a bottle warmer to bring red wine *up* to room temperature.

Last night on BBC television we saw a baby born before our eyes by Caesarean section in a London maternity hospital. The camera was placed next the surgeon's hands. As we watched the baby boy neatly lifted out and encouraged to breathe, the man at my right in the lounge swallowed hard— "My God, oh praise God"—in awe, not in horror.

This morning I saw in the London *Telegraph* that two little girls, aged nine and ten, also watched television to see their brother, named Mark, being born. When interviewed, the nine-year-old said, "I liked seeing Mark when he had no age at all. But I really like animal stories better."

Tonight on television we watched a kangaroo being born. The baby was one inch long, a blind worm making its long journey into the fur-lined pouch. Now I see why kangaroos are built that way—not a bad idea for a painless delivery. But for a human baby? Oh no. It would keep climbing back all its life into the warm airraid shelter. (Cyril Connolly says he is seeking a womb with a view.)

I'm glad to be getting an education on my sabbatical leave.

Coleridge came across an ass at Cambridge and addressed it in a tender poem, "To a Young Ass: Its Mother being tethered near it." (His first title I like better: "Monologue to a Young Jack Ass in Jesus Piece. Its mother near it chained to a log.")

The sweet glance of the miserable beast touched his heart. "Poor little foal of an oppresséd race!" he cried. "I love the languid Patience of thy face."

> I hail thee Brother—spite of the fool's scorn!
> And fain would take thee with me, in the Dell
> Of Peace and mild Equality to dwell.

What is *mild* equality, I wonder? The kind of brotherly love one feels for a jackass (though seemingly not for its mother).

Charles Lamb described these verses of Coleridge as "overtures of intimacy to a jackass."

Coleridge was twenty-two when he wrote the poem. Wordsworth was twenty-seven, living at Alfoxden three miles distant from Coleridge, when he came to share the same asinine fellowship and intoxication. In a note to "Peter Bell" he wrote, "In the woods of Alfoxden I used to take great delight in noticing the habits, tricks, and physiognomy of asses." Peter Bell, a brutal fellow indifferent to primroses, sees a solitary ass by moonlight turning its eyeball upon him, and, rebuked and transformed by the sight, he laments:

> When shall I be as good as thou?
> Oh! would, poor beast, that I had now
> A heart but half as good as thine!

Dorothy's Alfoxden Journal doesn't mention asses at all. She liked sheep.

THE ASSES OF ALFOXDEN

Fairest in the woodland passes
Were to him the little asses
Of Alfoxden—silvan creatures
Frolicking with their donkey features,
The long left ear aslant the head
That for the poet pivoted,
Braying in common with their kind
The burble of a windy mind
To which he harkened with delight.
And no one ever set him right.
A poet shouldn't stray so far
Where these Alfoxden asses are.

We took the day off and walked to Newmarket, ten miles from Cambridge. It's a thrilling place if you like jockeys and stud farms. There was a Jockey Training Ground for Gallops. An enormous sign on the highway said, "Beware racehorses"— a sensible rule of life, I think.

On the High Street, Newmarket, every shopkeeper's name was a monosyllable. What attraction—perhaps the racing life— had brought them all of a flock together? Crofts the fruiterer. Quant & Son, riding-out boots. Poole, cigars. Hobbs, ironmonger. Wigg & Son, silversmiths. Musk the butcher. Whipps, newspapers. Layngs, food and wine. Tooks the baker.

"I would have you see everything. It is a good way of getting knowledge, especially if you inquire carefully (as I hope you always do) after the meaning and the particulars of everything you see."
—Lord Chesterfield in a letter to his son.

Doomsday report from the London Sunday *Times,* a review of Brecht's play *Baal:* "The famous verses in which Brecht acridly compares life to a privy do really in this version, and as Peter O'Toole sings them, sound like poetry, as again does the tender and terrible song, a prelude to murder and homosexual frenzy, which Mr. O'Toole strums in the last act."

Brecht himself wrote of *Baal*, "I admit (and advise you) this play is lacking in wisdom."

David Ben Gurion, Yehudi Menuhin, Jawaharlal Nehru, and I have a solemn ritual in common: we stand daily on our heads. For survival.

A P R I L .   Coventry has a right to the symbol of the phoenix, having been consumed by fire and risen whole from the ashes (like D. H. Lawrence, who claimed the emblem for his own, and, for all I know, Phoenix, Arizona. I'd rather be a salamander and put out the fire). They overdo it. In the marketplace a phoenix is carved into the pavement; on a steel pole a gold phoenix sits. Above the blackened spire of St. Michael's Cathedral, the modern spire rises like a singed television aerial. Only Lady Godiva naked on a fine horse failed to remind me of a bird in flames.

When Coventry was bombed nearly out of existence, November 1940, the cathedral was gutted by a direct hit that sent the lead roof crashing into the nave. Next morning, someone picked from the ruins two charred beams and lashed them together to form a cross above the altar open to the sky.

The new cathedral, built as part of the destroyed one, takes us from fiery death (they say) to the resurrection and the life, past the charred cross through immense glass doors etched with shimmering white ghosts. The tremendous Christ at the new altar is, oddly, a tapestry, the largest in the world. But his white gown against vivid green is full and feminine, more a maid in a mead than a Christ Pantocrator. Clearly you can't weave passion into a tapestry.

On this Easter Monday, hundreds are lined up inching slowly forward under a sign "Queue up for Communion." The presence of the tourists agitates the people of Coventry. I read in the newspaper that 400 citizens have volunteered to kneel and pray in the cathedral at frequent intervals to give sightseers a notion of what the place is meant for. I wouldn't worry. A pleasure is as good as a prayer.

" 'Resurrection, Madam,' said the phoenix, 'is one of the most simple things in the world. There is nothing more astonishing in being born twice than once. Everything in this world is the effect of resurrection; caterpillars are regenerated into butterflies; a kernel put into the earth is regenerated into a tree.' "

—Voltaire, *The Princess of Babylon*

London is a roaring spectacle after sleepy Cambridge. But changed. At first it didn't seem different. In the White Hall, Bloomsbury Square, the night porter spent the night outside our door polishing the brass rail of the stairway. We had tea in the lounge along with 18 members of a Committee for Uplift, flushed and chatty after their meeting.

"Have you got your tea, Miss Fitch? Jolly good."

"This is Miss Briggs who's at Bristol. She does the students. Yes, yes, quite."

At the Museum pub, the Victorian bar was the same carved mahogany, its old-fashioned mirror spelling out in gold engraving "Watney and Co's Imperial Stout." Scotch eggs adorned the counter, sausages, herring, pickled onions. But a boy and girl were kissing in a hot embrace at the table beside us.

England is changed. This is the era of noisy little people, "The Small World of Sammy Lee" (a London film). On stage and BBC, the defiant characters are bus drivers, coal miners, angry young millhands. They speak a murderous Cockney or Midland dialect, "bloody" sore at everybody, howling in discontent, demanding to be heard. To ease their bloody feelings they hop into bed and get a girl pregnant, more likely two girls. It takes two these days.

Tonight at the theater, the plotless play "Next Time I'll Sing to You" was about *not* being a play, with four men and a girl in baggy sweaters and tight pants. "If there is a point," they said, "this is beside the point." They had in mind, if anything, man's inescapable solitude (nobody slept with the girl). This may be Auden's "Age of Anxiety" fifteen years later—his poem had three men and a girl nobody slept with. But they sounded more like quitters than like Auden's failures, more like hostile little people, inarticulate, unwashed, and boring.

V. S. Pritchett calls London "the least nervous city in the world" with calm on her face. And all that traffic roaring on the left?

Across the street from our hotel, the little park in Bloomsbury Square blazes with red tulips, pigeons, and lovers. It boasts a single statue, Charles James Fox in a stone toga and sandals, a roll of Magna Carta in his right hand—the noblest Londoner of them all (some Londoners would have said the ignoblest). He possessed all the talents, such as universal knowledge and benevolence of heart, was a magnificent rake, a famous wit, a great politician. His habit of drinking and gambling all night led his father, Lord Holland, to say when his son was to be married, "At any rate, Charles will spend one night in bed." Horace Walpole wrote, "He was as little disagreeable as such overbearing presumption could allow." George III said, "He is as contemptible as he is odious."

Princess Alexandra has married a commoner, Mr. Angus Ogilvy ("My ain luv," according to the tabloids), and gone to live humbly in Thatched House Lodge, Richmond Park. It has a slate roof. After the wedding ceremony in Westminster Abbey (shown on BBC), Queen Elizabeth waiting with impatience for her car trod smack on the foot of the King of Norway. "I beg your pardon," she said, not "I beg Your Majesty's pardon," as Mr. Ogilvy would have to say.

As I waited at the bus stop at Oxford Circus, a young man fled past, followed by an incensed woman who stopped short in front of me. "Ah-ow-ow-oo!" said Eliza Doolittle, waving her arms in fury, "did you hear the language that young smarty used before me very face? A stream of dirty words it was, right in me bloody face! 'I'll put you in charge,' I says to him, 'using such talk in front of a lady.' In public, too!"

"I didn't hear him," I told her.

"Then all I say is, bully for you you didn't!"

M A Y .   From Kings Cross this morning, we went by train
to Yorkshire. The countryside has become May, willow green
with gold celandine. Spring in England is three months
behind Greece.

At Leeds, Quentin Bell's Pre-Raphaelite beard was brightly
visible among the crowds on the station platform. The Bells
live at the edge of town. We dashed into a concealed entrance
to their lane, where a large sign gave welcome: "Highthorne
House DANGER," the last word in huge red letters, plainly an
approach to Hell (abandon hope). But since Quentin ignored
it I assumed the danger wasn't immediate. Inside the courtyard, the stone house and lily pool looked safe, also the gray
concrete lady whom Quentin had recently molded and cast.

Quentin's wife Olivier (her mother's maiden name) is lovely,
the daughter of Hugh Popham, Keeper of Prints at the British
Museum, who is visiting the Bells this weekend. Her mother
was Brynhild Olivier, a famous beauty of Bloomsbury. Years
ago, after her parents were divorced, young Olivier was sent
abroad to boarding school, feeling dull and unwanted. On her
return, she joined a small acting group, after which she summoned courage to write her first cousin, Laurence Olivier, to
ask for a part. His secretary replied curtly that Mr. Olivier
was out of town. She never tried again.

With such parents and antecedents, the three children of
Quentin Bell are as I imagine Leslie Stephen's children were
at their age. (Vanessa Stephen became Quentin's mother;
Virginia became Virginia Woolf.) Julian Bell, now ten, is
named for Vanessa's son and Quentin's brother killed in the
Spanish Civil War. Virginia Bell at seven is incredibly like, a
replica of, Virginia Woolf, with a thin delicate face, long
straight hair, perfect manners, and wilful spirit. The youngest,
turned four, is Cressida. You hear no sound of Yorkshire in
their speech. Their home, full of pictures and books, is worn
and littered, with a carelessness I associate with a leaning to
the arts. Quentin makes exquisite pottery for their meals, but
it chips easily; he likes it chipped. In our room is a large
portrait of Virginia Woolf painted by Vanessa. Quentin, historian of Bloomsbury whose ghosts may shudder a little, is writing a biography of his aunt Virginia. Its candor worries him.

After tea the eight of us played a game they call "Russian Pictures" (more like Russian roulette), the most humiliating parlor game I've ever sweated through. I don't mind writing an occasional *bout-rimé* sonnet to please my hostess if her taste runs to such antics, but I almost broke down and wept at this test of skill.

First you think of a famous painting (a Titian, a Modigliani) and write only its title at the top of a long sheet of paper. The person next to you reads the title and draws a quick *sketch*, recalling perfectly the original. The paper is folded to hide the title. The third person studies the sketch and adds the correct title beneath or, if unable to recognize it (he ought to) chooses an appropriate title to give it. The fourth person draws a picture to fit the new title, and so on as long as the paper holds out.

I grasped the rules all right. But the pictures I was asked to draw or recognize had such titles as "Ariadne in Naxos," "The Murder of Agamemnon," and "Dignity and Impudence." The children were clever at this simple game (Cressida at four was about my speed). When I put Ariadne on a promontory, having no idea what she was doing at the moment in Naxos, Quentin cried out indignantly, "*Who* drew this?" To a sketch of "Nude Descending a Staircase," in wild despair I gave the title "The Blessed Damozel," and for that bit of originality received loud praise.

In Yorkshire weather, foggy, rainy, cold, we had a family picnic at Fountains Abbey. We went in two cars, stopping part way to consult the map, at Ripon, where Mr. Popham spied a small Anglican church. "I do like to step inside a church," he said, leading the way as a confirmed critic of historical relics. It was a new experience for the children, totally unacquainted with churches. As we walked down the empty aisle, Virginia asked, "What is that up ahead?" "It's an altar, darling," her mother said. Cressida clamored to be shown. "Smashing," she said. "Is it for flowers?"

On the greensward at Fountains Abbey, we ate sausage sandwiches and drank stout among the damp forgetmenots and celandines. The children raced over the monastic ruins of the Abbey, begun by thirteen Cistercian monks in 1132 and laid to destruction by Henry VIII. Since Quentin assumes my shrines are literary, he recommended this one by calling it a close reproduction of Mr. Darcy's estate. "If you block out the ruins," he said.

Quentin refused to show us the University of Leeds, where he is professor of art—too redbrick and ugly (yet when he visited us in North Carolina we showed him Duke without hesitation, allowing him the freedom of his opinion). Tonight the Leeds professors came to dinner, Quentin wearing the same old brown sweater he had worn all day. I disarmed Mr. Norman Jeffares by guessing that by now five hundred students of mine had read his book on Yeats, a fact he found endearing. He, like the rest, was unquenchably anecdotal, and I marveled once again why a dinner guest feels obliged to keep talking. It must be better than bleak silence. Even the great diner-out Sydney Smith probably chattered on and on, his wit only intermittent.

Back in London, this morning after breakfast B. and I started for Regent Street to buy gifts to take home. "We'll need money," B. said. I unlocked a suitcase to remove some traveler's checks and cash. They were gone. So was my diamond pendant. The loss, we realized, amounted to a thousand dollars.

Within a half hour, Scotland Yard was at the door in the person of Sergeant Gibson, just stepped from a role in a murder mystery. He wore a belted trench coat with turned-up collar, an air of having solved worse cases. His speech was clipped, his eyes steely. Summoning three chambermaids and two housemen (no butler, no reporter from The Times), he interviewed them and us in a courteous, brisk manner. We were caught in a Sayers novel but provided no clues. Nobody burst into tears and confessed the crime.

Sergeant Gibson, pipe in mouth, notebook in hand, loped off to the American Express to report the missing checks. We followed. By noon Mr. Mountfort, former C.I.D. man, had restored the amount of the checks. He said, "Are you willing

to fly back from the States to testify when we catch the thief?"
"No," I said. Mr. Mountfort thanked me for a firm answer. The
interview was cordial, low-keyed. We shook hands, went on
to Liberty's and shopped.

We have been watched as we came and went, says Mr.
Toppo, the hotel manager. I feel the old English draft on the
back of my neck. At least fifty people have access to our
room, since the hotel uses large skeleton keys. In so respectable
a hotel, genteel, safe, and now aghast, a thief is unthinkable.
It would happen to Americans. We have lowered the tone.

I asked B., "Well, what philosophy?" "Just a nuisance," he
said.

This is Derby Day, May 29. My theory is that a reasonable
man bets on the favorite, since it is likely to win. B. patiently
explained.

"But that's unsporting, love."

"What is?"

"To bet on a sure thing."

At the local pub they were betting on the 100-to-one shot.
So was B. Today the favorite won.

F. L. Lucas says the Shah of Persia was once invited to
watch the Derby during a visit to England. He refused, since
he already knew that if a number of horses ran the same way
at the same time one would run faster than the others. He
didn't care which.

JUNE. The life preserver beside my deckchair says,
"S.S. United States—New York." This may not be American
soil, but it's an American sea. We are on the largest swiftest
superliner afloat to take us home. My only regret is that afternoon tea is served in tea bags.

Last night the ship went into stormy weather with a roll
that, in the night, sent the articles on the chest between our
beds tumbling downhill into mine. Two glasses of water
poured into my face. The telephone (why have we a telephone?) slid to the edge and stopped, but six books and a

bowl of oranges kept on coming. A voice in the corridor cried, "May I have some pink pills, please?"

Today the lines are strung up to hold to, for those on their feet. B. and I have strong stomachs, else we would have avoided ships long ago. Mine is strong enough for reading Simone de Beauvoir, *Memoirs of a Dutiful Daughter*. She told Jacques (at eighteen) of her boredom, how she no longer saw any meaning to life. "There's no need to look so hard," he said.

The children's movie is "Gunman from Loredo." Meanwhile we skim the rough water in a motor boat. Last August, the bar man says, the ship went through a hurricane at top speed (50 m.p.h.). "Yipes! were the passengers scared!" At dinner tonight little American flags marked each place, while the orchestra played "Yankee Doodle" and "God Bless America." On this crossing a foreigner, having been introduced to the United States and our native tribal customs, can turn around and go home.

This morning the taxi in New York took us past the dock where the *Vulcania* waited with steam up, ready to sail this very noon, June 5. If we were indeed lost souls, we might go aboard her to start over again. Like Sisyphus.

I want to go home! B.'s headaches, which began before we left London, are constant and severe, though he calls it nothing but eyestrain. On the Silver Star to Raleigh (why didn't I insist that we fly, get him to a doctor?), through a countryside lacking chimneypots and hedgerows, we returned mile by slow mile of track to the South. I heard a Southern lady say in drawling tones to the conductor, "Sir, I declare I am about to pay you a compliment." So gracious a preamble gives one time to brace oneself.

The telephone was ringing, David from Charlottesville, "May we come tonight?" They arrived at 2:00 A.M., bringing the new Philip, born while we were in London. Surrounded by laughing faces, he was an armful of miracle to meet in the dead of night. He has what President Kennedy calls vigah.

June 24. B. was operated on today at Duke Hospital. A brain tumor. A malignancy.

Somewhere E. B. White says, "For me, the scene has been spoiled by the maggots that work in the mind." The maggots are at work in B.'s mind, and they work in mine.

Thoreau and Mr. White of Selborne wrote daily journals, filling many pages, many volumes. Yet they never recorded bad news—as if there were none possible in their lives. I think they saw no good to anyone in setting down the terrible untellable part.

AUGUST. These summer days I'm reading aloud to B.—as he lies on the chaise longue on the porch—a biography of Maria Theresa (the lady who always met a European crisis while pregnant, who had sixteen children including Marie Antoinette and a palace of 1,441 rooms), but not including the ending, her death scene. I've omitted that. He doesn't appear to notice. On her deathbed, when her son Joseph said to her in her pain, "You are not at ease," Maria Theresa's last words were, "I am sufficiently at my ease to die."

Why were we taught to believe in happy endings? A biography can have no happy ending, since it is a life—the flat contradiction of the fairytale. It might be called a mortality. ("I find it won't do," said the Duchess of Argyle, dying. "Desire the Duke to leave the room.") Maria Theresa survived for sixty-three years without flagging. She was B.'s age.

I'm reading to him Dr. Johnson's *Dictionary*, because B. likes reading any book from A to Z. I skip around to find laughable words, name-calling and abusive words: *bellygod* for a glutton. *fub* for a chubby boy. *ninnyhammer*, a simpleton. *pickleherring*, a jack-pudding or buffoon. *sinworm*, a vile creature. *smellfeast*, a parasite. *stinkard*, a mean stinking paltry fellow. *tonguepad*, a great talker. *trubtail*, a short squat woman. *wittol*, a tame cuckold. *yux*, the hiccough.

"I am not answerable for all the words in my Dictionary," Dr. Johnson told Boswell. He omitted a few: *smellsmock* (which is in Rabelais) for a licentious man, though he included *smicket*, a woman's smock. Put the two together and you have a brand new word—*smellsmicket.*

Name-calling:

Sydney Smith called Macaulay "a book in britches."

Macaulay called Horace Walpole "a heartless fribble."

Horace Walpole called Lady Mary Montagu "an old, foul, tawdry, painted, plastered personage."

Lady Mary Montagu called Pope a murderer, "Mark'd on thy back, like Cain, by God's own hand."

Pope called Lady Mary a whore, "As who knows Sappho, smiles at other whores."

Lady Mary called Horace Walpole—let's see—

More name-calling:

"Sir bolninge bowde [Sir swollen malt-weevil]"   —*The Castle of Perseverence*

"Thou blynkerd blowball."   —Skelton

"Ye brainsick fools, ye hoddypeaks, ye doddypoles."   —Hugh Latimer, in a sermon before Edward VI

"Out of my door, you witch, you hag, you baggage, you polecat, you ronyon! out, out!"   —*Merry Wives of Windsor*

"Away, rubbish . . . Avaunt, kitchen-stuff! Rip, you brown-bread Tannikin; out of my sight! . . . hence, you hopperarse! you barley-pudding, full of maggots!"   —Thomas Dekker, *The Shoemakers' Holiday*

"You slawsy poodle, you tike,
   You crapulous puddering pip-squeak."
   —Christopher Fry, *The Lady's Not for Burning*

Fools, sots, buffoons,
Dolts, noodles, loons—
Mere names to call
But true withal.

SEPTEMBER. Philip my son is moving to California to teach nuclear physics at Stanford. Yesterday the children came down the dirt road one time more, Ann at five and Mark at almost three, his legs keeping up like scissors, never to meet me from that house again. I wept in my heart "never, never," then stopped for shame. It is unseemly to weep when they want to go. Soon we were racing through the house, drinking lemonade. "It's summer," Ann cried. "Let's do summersaults."

And today Philip said smiling "Goodbye, Mama," and they drove off to California in their station wagon (better than a covered wagon). The huge moving van was at the door; by mid-afternoon it was gone. My stricken mind said, "Their house is empty." But my eyes said, "Oh, no!" Joan had forgot her silken wedding dress as well as hundreds and hundreds of fragile Christmas tree ornaments.

B. and I returned together to our teaching this September. I don't think I could have gone back without him. I don't believe either of us could have managed it alone. He had to live.

The ordeal of entering a classroom after fifteen months was soon over. I made a brave splash, full of sound and visibility (taking the Maid of Orléans' line: I am a mere farmhand but to me has been revealed the word of God). I told them poetry is useful, and they wrote it gravely into their notebooks. But is poetry still alive? The modern poets were swarming in the flesh when I began teaching, all except Yeats. This year Frost, Cummings, William Carlos Williams, Theodore Roethke, and Louis MacNeice spoke no more. Some like Pound have been unalive for years.

The question is not will poetry survive. Of course it will. (Horace Walpole announced in 1744, "Pope and poetry are dead." Only Pope was.) But shall we survive? Of course not. We happen to be caught in a temporarily nonpoetic time, full of wasteland noises and tunelessness. Any day now, I hope, one, *one* new honest-to-God poet will turn up before I have to stop looking for him.

OCTOBER.   *The Miseries of Human Life* by James Beresford, an English country parson (unmarried) who in 1806 sat down to address The Miserable, is in twelve plaintive dialogues. His characters Timothy Testy and Samuel Sensitive grieve and groan while Mrs. Testy sighs beside them and the baby howls with a dry wet nurse.

"O, horrible! O, horrible! most horrible," cries Sensitive, like the Ghost in *Hamlet*.

"O, horror, horror, horror, horror, horror!" echoes Testy, a blighted man.

They endear to me the rains of October. They deal with the minor woes of life: the weather, the social blunders, pricks, passing embarrassments, mortifications that dampen a person's days. The Rev. Mr. Beresford had a talent for little calamities and small drizzles, good to read in these squally times. No deluge ever happened to him, nothing of significance or import. Only chagrin. He spent his life being made to look and feel like a fool. And his readers, in perfect sympathy, demanded a second volume.

"Compose yourself, Mr. Testy," begs Sensitive, shuddering to recall:

"Feeling your foot slidder over the back of a toad, which you took for a stepping stone, in your dark evening walk."

"Missing the way to your mouth and drowning your breast in a bath of beer."

"Sitting in a chair on which you do not discover that honey

has been liberally spilt till, in rising to make your bow, you
carry away the cushion."

NOVEMBER. This morning early the telephone rang.
Francis Brown, editor of the New York *Times Book Review,*
said cheerily from New York, "Hello, I've forgotten completely
about Christmas." "So have I," I said.

He asked me to write a verse for the first page of the
Review and, because of short notice, write it in one week in
14 lines. I need only pay tribute to books, advise people to
buy them, and wish everyone a merry Christmas. "Why don't
I just dictate a sonnet over the phone," I said. I didn't tell
him my verse comes by the yard, and 14 lines take longer
to write than 40.

Two years ago the Duke students hired speakers for a three-
day forum on the Post-Christian Man. This year the subject is
the Post-Human Man. As a sample of the type, tonight we
heard the poet W. D. Snodgrass.

I should think a post-human man would be a dead one. But
labeling himself a counter-revolutionary, Snodgrass announced
that poets are making a return to the world (wherever they
may have been till now), to questions of sex, marriage, divorce,
business. "We live by our physical senses," he said, and the
result is evidently uninspiring, the poetry commonsensical,
ordinary, a lowering of tone and voltage. No ecstasy.

"I want my poems to be even silly in places," he said, a
curious ambition but one easy to achieve. He advised the
students, "You don't need *more* experience, you need *less.*
Experience deadens you so that you become like people who
go to bed with everybody because they can't feel anything."
(I couldn't follow that logic.) The post-human man is not
unlike the pre-human man. A Darwinian poet, Snodgrass. I
wouldn't call him a monkey.

I came home disheartened and read an interview with T. S.
Eliot in the *Paris Review.* "No," said Mr. Eliot, "I don't see
anything that looks to me like a counter-revolution."

November 22. In the midst of weighing a pound of string beans at the A. & P., I turned to see B.'s anguished face streaming with tears. "A terrible thing has happened," he whispered. "They killed John Kennedy."

A man came up behind B. "He was shot an hour ago in Texas," he said. "The chapel bell at Duke is tolling."

On Sunday morning we sat motionless before the television screen, with a clear view of the grief of the world. As the picture shifted from the White House and the President's coffin to the city jail of Dallas, Texas, a murder occurred—a second murder—when Lee Harvey Oswald, 24, was shot by Jack Ruby, a Dallas night club owner. As eye witnesses to death and hate and terror, we who ought to testify couldn't even cry out. Our peril is great. We are all involved, the violence is in us all. When we reach rock bottom, where is there to go?

D E C E M B E R .   My verse appeared on the front page of the New York *Times Book Review* on schedule, but the timing was wrong. It was too light a piece, wrong in tone for a period of national mourning, personal mourning. The magazine had gone to press before the tragedy. I looked at it in tears.

And yet the verse was built on Yeats's questioning line: " 'What then?' sang Plato's ghost. 'What then?' " The ghost mocks our mortal undertakings. And along comes the witch.

1964

JANUARY.   I heard a news report today that automation is one of the major problems of 1964, a force expected to change things for the worse. In our private life, B.'s and mine, it isn't much of a problem. We aren't automated so far, with few electronic devices for the good life and no desire whatever to change. Ours is a human problem of holding on dearly to life itself.

A student told me after class that last August, when she waited on table in a hotel in Wisconsin, she served a handsome middleaged man who asked her, "Do you happen to know Helen Bevington? I used to be her boyfriend. Please give her my love."

"What was his name?"

"Oh, he didn't tell me his name," she replied, looking blank. "Did you have, I mean, is there *another* one?"

Lancelot Brown is an inspiring man, born in Northumberland in 1716. A gardener of England's finest estates, he used to change pasture lands into parks by recognizing the "capabilities," and was known thereafter as Capability Brown. Everybody's estate, he said, had a great capability of improvement.

He was a man of vistas, prospects, sweeping lawns, cascades and waterfalls. He wiped out many an old formal garden in favor of a natural look and was angrily accused of copying nature, a habit many disapproved of and considered vulgar. Though he planted more than a million trees, he also thinned them out for his vistas and so was damned as a destroyer. His masterpiece was the park at Blenheim. When he died they said he went to improve the Elysian fields.

The more famed Capability Brown grew, the more ha-ha's he hastened to dig. *Ha-ha* comes from ha! ha!, an exclamation of stunned surprise made by anybody happening to fall into one. It was nearly invisible, a ditch or sunk fence (to keep

cows and sheep from gazing in the windows), arranged so
cunningly that, with your eye on the distant expanse, you
tended to notice it just too late. I wish Gainsborough had
painted the scene. Or better, Hogarth.

> Vistas I love and gardeners at Kew
> Like Capability Brown, whom England knew
> As digger of the ha-ha, a small ditch
> In place of a garden wall to spoil the view.
> When each rapt visitor cried "Ha! ha!" which
> Meant only he was so engrossed at Kew
> In vistas, around 1752,
> That happily he'd fallen flat in a ditch—

> Capability Brown, aware that prospects please,
> Saw in the ha-ha capabilities.

FEBRUARY.   Archytas (a friend of Plato's) is supposed to have invented the screw and the pulley, for which
nobody remembers him. His other gift to mankind was a
wooden dove that could fly. Yeats made a mechanical golden
bird that could sing, "Of hammered gold and gold enamel-
ling / To keep a drowsy Emperor awake." Anything in that
line is worth trying.

SONGBIRDS

> Archytas made a wooden dove, and it could fly.
> Yeats set a gold-enamelled bird upon a golden bough.
>   And I (ornithologist of birds
> Goldwrought, woodwrought, wrought of words)
> Know they can sing as turtledove and cuckoo can
> And soar like wild umbrella birds
> And screech like forests of toucan,
> Since the artificer is man.

The longhaired Beatles from Liverpool are our latest song-
birds, or Beatlebirds, who rock and roll on the Ed Sullivan
show. "I Want to Hold Your Hand," they sing, and the planet
begins to rumble off its axis again. It is the listeners who really
frighten me, screaming their lungs out—primal screams.

I prayed for snow tonight. I said to Rosa as she cleaned the
house, "It's a good thing I have no influence with God," a
remark that unglued her. She leaned on her broom, muttering
it over, chuckling, then with a sigh said, "Well, I must get back
to my rat killing."

But the night stayed clear. We had to go after all to hear a
visiting critic, Denis Donoghue, air his views on Wallace
Stevens, William Carlos Williams, and Robert Frost. I thought
the Irish Mr. Donoghue must be studying for the priesthood
(turned out he has six children), a solemn man, unaware of
a shred of wit in his poets, detecting only gravity. I think they
have wit. By heaven, I hope so. The Comic Spirit is spurned
these days, unfashionable, unrecognized even when it walks up
to shake hands. To regard life lightly is not in mode, certainly
to countenance lightness in poets is not. As Rosa says, of things
in general, "It's hectifying."

Fortunately I wore around my neck on a gold chain my
great-grandmother's gold watch, which I cupped in my hands
and held hidden to my ear. The tick is a great comfort at such
times, the loud steady tick of Narcissa Spaulding's timepiece.
I never met her. She was listening to it a hundred years ago,
pinned to her breast over her heart, and I hope she smiled
bravely at the orators she heard, knowing how time was a-
wasting.

Yesterday a student asked a reasonable question after reading some modern critics: "How can you deal with passion in
dispassionate prose?" How can you deal with wit in dull
sobriety? The answer is, you can't, but people do.

Toulouse-Lautrec: "Without wit, I'd be an utter fool." Poor
sawed-off Lautrec: he was what brevity is the soul of. Yet
there is sense in Augustine Birrell's comment to a boastful
man: "If you tell me you are witty, I must trouble you to make
a joke."

MARCH.   The March days stir one to think heraldic:
or, argent, blanc, sable, gules, jaune, azure, vert, purpure—
lovely names. All nine are here on time. I wonder how many
blazoning colors will fit into a versicle.

> I go in blanc and sable
> (What a God's name so meek for?)
> Now the sky has turned heraldic
> In or and argent weather.
> Vert are the trees, emblazoned
> Bearings on the escutcheon,
> Jaune are the daffodils,
> The iris become pure purpure.
> I walk here passant gardant,
> Gules in the face, my tinctures
> Bright on the fields of azure.

David and Peggy, disfigured and scourged by poison ivy as
a result of a backlot enterprise, are led to ponder the existence
of evil. "Was poison ivy created in the first six days? Why?
Was it placed by the Lord in the Garden of Eden to flourish
along with the innocent roses and white lilies? Was it poison-
ous from the start, or did the poison come (like sin and death)
with the fall of man? Did Adam suffer a rash from it? If
this poison ivy was indeed created by God and not by the
devil's cunning, am I to think him a just God?"

APRIL.   I'm taking my annual spring trip with the
students through the *Four Quartets*, an exhausting journey (or
footrace) from world drought in quest of peace, and in Eliot's
cruellest month too. The same fear haunts me as I stare at the
whirling clock I'll never make it there and back. I teach by
clock ticks: fifty minutes to eternity and return before lunch,
which is more than Eliot had to do on an empty stomach. Each
year we chase round and round on the circular scenic tour, a
whisk on the Wheel, hurtling through time, missing salvation

altogether. Personally I've never come anywhere near the stopping place, the serene center and the peace that passeth understanding. Nor so far has a student said, "Stop the Wheel, I want to get off."

The Panama Canal was completed eight years after my birth. I'm three years older than the Model T Ford, which has become obsolete. Today I finished the book about Charley. Having begun at a starting point (my birth), I came to a stopping place (his death).

I wrote it for survival. I wrote it to keep my sanity intact, if possible, while B. lives. Now the book exists, whatever may be said of my faculties. But how long have we left? How long will he survive?

MAY.   B. collapsed in his office and barely reached home, driving alone and hardly conscious, his mind distrait, fragmented. He had taught a class in *Paradise Lost* (forever lost) to the end of the hour, stumbled to his office, tried to telephone for help. He had forgotten how to dial, how to read numbers, how to spell his doctor's name. Almost blind, almost mindless, he ran down the stairs and drove six miles home to me, thinking only of reaching me. When I went to school the next day to teach his classes, as he told me I must, his students were weeping in the hall.

We've lived on the edge of a volcano that finally erupted, the same hot volcano for five years. It came to have the air and semblance of home. For five years I've known he must die of cancer. The only question was, how soon? I love him and thank him for surviving so long.

I think he did not know. He had no reason not to hope after the first operation, for as far as he was told the prognosis was good. But the time was always too late. I write it down now because he cannot read it, can never read again.

Princess, it is as if one take away
Green woods from forests, and sunshine from the day.

SEPTEMBER.   He has been dead for five weeks, counting from 11:00 this morning. I had expected grief, but not panic, not sheer terror. I miss him beyond belief or reason, beyond the will to live.

One of the last things I read to him was the manuscript about Charley, because he asked me to. He seemed to follow much of it and to understand. He said as far as he had known my father, the story I told was true. Once when I choked, he said, "I'm glad those tears aren't for me." But they were for him, for me, for Charley who is dead, for the world of mortal men. And now, like Lizzie before me, I am alone.

There are no guarantees. What happens, happens.

OCTOBER.   Eleanor looks into my face and says, "You're desperate, aren't you?" (Held together, she says most of us are, with paper clips and Scotch tape.) Her voice is professional, a doctor's voice.

I finally began to write today, two months later. Isak Dinesen said, "All sorrows can be borne if you put them into a story or tell a story about them." This is a love story about B. to even things up between us, of a time over and done for both of us, when we were alive and young together. So far I know only the title: *A Book and a Love Affair.* That sums it up.

With him I came first in his life, as he came first in mine. Now I'm not first with anyone at all. And can never be. The panic comes from the realization.

Camus: "Knowing whether one can live *without appeal* is all that interests me." One day at a time, B. said. But he forgot to tell me how to live the nights.

Montesquieu, when his sight was failing, said, "I know how to be blind." Maybe when life wanes one can say, "I know how to be a ghost." It seems accommodating, not morbid, to think of myself as a ghost. A ghost expects to be solitary, and I imagine bored. It can't afford to look for human love beyond its deserts. A ghost must learn its place and not haunt people. I don't feel like a survivor. I feel left behind.

Kate the Bold is born at last, the much-wanted, much-loved Kate who twice before was expected and twice chose the glory of being male. David likes her female, though last night before Peggy went to the hospital and the two little boys were shrieking, he remarked, "I don't care whether this baby is a boy or a girl, but I think it should have a very small v₋ice."

I went to Charlottesville for the weekend to see Kate, by Trailways bus (not trusting myself to drive), but I should never have gone. Not yet. I arrived weeping on their doorstep, weeping made it back home. It was a blight on their happiness—a time to be born, not a time to die.

I can't find the words to write the story of B. How can I, when he is dead? I don't know the language for him. Colette told about her father, who planned to write a book, some immense work on the French army. He finished the first page, three words of dedication to his wife: *ma chère âme*. At his death they found in his library twelve bound volumes filled with hundreds, thousands of sheets of paper. Except for those three loving words, the pages were blank.

Two mice fell into a pail of cream. One drowned. The other kept on struggling till the cream churned into butter and he climbed out.

Or one might say it Auden's way, "with prolonged drowning to develop gills."

So many images of drowning. In the *Ars Poetica* Horace tells of a man who falls into a deep well. He cries for help but nobody ever comes to pull him out for, as all agree, he may have done it on purpose.

NOVEMBER.   I ask people who have tried it how to live alone. I asked a professor's wife at Duke, a widow these three years. She burst into sobs. "It can't be done," she said.

I asked a professor, a widower for ten years. He said, "Try martinis." Another friend puts beside her bed a flashlight, a cow bell, and a barking dog.

Books will tell me. Montaigne and Thoreau agreed on the virtue of being alone. No talk of loneliness from them. They liked their independence and privacy.

Montaigne wanted an *arrière-boutique,* all his own, all free, to "live really alone and to live that way contentedly." His tower was his retreat: "There is my throne. I try to make my authority over it absolute, and to withdraw this one corner from all society. . . . I find it measurably more endurable to be always alone than never to be able to be alone." But his mother, wife, child, servants were nearby, right downstairs.

Thoreau said again and again: "I love to be alone." "I have an immense appetite for solitude." "I thrive best on solitude." "I believe there is no man who will not, comparatively speaking, spoil my afternoon." But he could always walk home the two miles to Concord for a piece of his mother's apple pie.

Sydney Smith wrote: "Living a great deal alone (as I now do) will, I believe, correct me of my faults, for a man can do without his own approbation in much society, but he must make great exertions to gain it when he is alone; without it, I am convinced, solitude is not to be endured." But his loved and loving wife shared his bed and outlived him.

Camus wasn't so sure. He wrote like a comfortless man. In the *Notebooks* (1942–1951), the first words are: "Whatever does not kill me strengthens me. Yes, but—" The problem to be solved practically was this: can one be happy and solitary? Can one live without bitterness? He answered himself: "I had shouted, demanded, exulted, despaired. But at the age of thirty-seven one day I made the acquaintance of misfortune and found out what, despite appearances, I had not known until then. Around the middle of my life I had to learn all over again painfully how to live alone."

The idea is to be one's own best friend. Anyone who knows himself, says Montaigne, loves and cultivates himself before anything else. (To Helen, with love and squalor.)

Yet I admit what is the real disadvantage of such advice—

these are all *dead* men who would tell me how to live. Men of wit and courage, their only failure in eloquence is to be dead.

> No shade, no shine, no butterflies, no bees,
> No fruits, no flowers, no leaves, no birds—November!

The November poet is Thomas Hood, born a Londoner, dead a Londoner, buried in Kensal Green. Of the world beyond Fleet Street he sounds misinformed. I look around me this morning and catch sight of a yellow butterfly crossing the dooryard. A dozen grackles and starlings are strung like clothespins on the telephone wire. In bright sun, gold leaves fall from the maples and hickories, chrysanthemums bloom in the garden. Tomorrow the white buds of the camellia will open outside my window. November!

I think Thomas Hood should have hopped over to Hampshire to correct his poem. Mr. White of Selborne kept a journal full of Novembers, of redwings and redbreasts, rooks, stonecurlews, stone-chats, larks, plovers, martins, titmice, hedge sparrows, and wild wood pigeons; of chrysanthemums, nasturtiums, pinks and cloves . . .

Nov. 2, 1769.   Golden-crowned wren on the tops of trees.
Nov. 14, 1770. Bee on the asters.
Nov. 19, 1773. Gathered in the grapes.
Nov. 3, 1777.   Beetles fly.
Nov. 26, 1791. Three gallons of brandy from London.
Nov. 5, 1792.   Gossamer abounds.

DECEMBER.   "I have a passion for the truth, and for the fictions that it authorizes." Jules Renard said that. I keep thinking of it as I write about falling in love with B. The truth, the fictions.

In *The Mayor of Casterbridge* (which I must teach next term), Hardy remarks of Farfrae, after his wife's death, that he was able to estimate their love, "all that it was, and all that it was not." He was a rare unraveller, undeceived by loss. I can tell, in part, what love *was*. I can't remember what it was not.

At a Christmas party I met Memory Lester, who now lives in Chapel Hill. Oh, Mrs. Lester. She worked as a desk clerk at the Carpenter Library at Columbia when B. and I were graduate students, falling in love daily before her eyes. Memory has lost her memory of our love story. I peered into her pretty face today, recalling how jealous I was, how I despaired of that prettiness once. She was a flirt, and B. would laugh if he could see her again, and she would still flirt with him but I wouldn't be jealous. I would take him home.

This year has had 366 days. Not to save my soul would I live any one of them again.

Sydney Smith's advice: "Short views of human life—not further than dinner or tea." (But I was born Helen Smith, not Sydney. I haven't yet shortened my views.) And Hopkins's: "Patience—hard thing." What is harder, more beyond reach, than patience?

I write even on Sunday now (instead of falling on my face). And I don't know where my next word is coming from.

1965

JANUARY. Sartre ends his autobiography, *The Words:*
"My sole concern has been to save myself—nothing in my
hands, nothing up my sleeve—by work and faith. . . . Without equipment, without tools, I set all of me to work in order
to save all of me."

Everybody, even Sartre, is concerned with survival, the
word for our time. An Existentialist wants to exist.

T. S. Eliot started off 1965 by dying on Monday. (Dorothy
Parker: "My Lord, how people die!") I'm sorry about Eliot.
His death affects my life, puts the present back inexorably
into the past. Also, as he must have known, he had a number
of things to clear up and straighten out, lest he be forever mis-
understood. He had obligations to himself, like clarity. To say
"It means whatever it means to you" was a tiresome evasion.
A poem means what it says.

So the diffident young man he had been betrayed him; the
old man he became kept to the last a capricious humor. Now
East Coker, both the poem and the place (of his forefathers)
where he is buried, witness his death, "In my beginning is my
end." Let his poetry live on to make him immortal so that the
rest of his claim may also prove true, "In my end is my
beginning."

Frances Gray Patton, Reynolds Price, and I sat in a row on
the platform at Hill House to entertain the faculty wives this
morning after breakfast. It was one of those Panels—to talk
loosely about writing. The improvisation was nonsense, the
information useless. Yet, as their questions showed, the ladies
not only were goodnatured to come and listen but sought to
put us at ease.

"Do you have an agent?" I was asked.

"No."

"Do you use a typewriter?"

"Yes."

I thought we were, if anything, comical, though Reynolds as a young dedicated writer sounded in earnest. Fanny was delightful, giving the occasion its due. She said she liked to think she was inspired by God.

Inspired, she could have told them, like Alfred Austin, poet laureate at the turn of the century. When some grammatical mistakes in his poems were pointed out to him, he replied, "I dare not alter these things. They come to me from above."

Alfred Austin referred to his celestial inspiration or Muse as "It." Only once "It" abandoned him, just after he had written the lines:

> As for the twain they vanished in the rattle
> Of jolting tumbrils and the joy of battle.

Heaven was understandably silenced, floored by a couplet. In due time "It" returned, and Austin went on writing some of the worst verse on record.

FEBRUARY.   I said to Eleanor, who was listing her own survival problems, "I always wish on a star."

"What do you wish?"

"I wish for a solution."

How to maintain hope, that's the question. Paul Tillich said, "Hope is easy for the foolish, hard for the wise"—the only proof one has of a degree of wisdom.

Today in a ceremony in the Rare Book Room of Duke University Library, the English graduate students gave a first edition of *Middlemarch* to the library in B.'s name. They had no way of knowing it was the last book I read to him, the final tale we heard together. He knew it very well. He liked even its longwindedness and laughed at its Victorian humor (Mrs. Cadwallader: "These charitable people never know vinegar from wine till they have swallowed it and got the colic").

I read on day after day and never finished. At last I looked

up from the page and he had stopped listening. He became
unaware, then unconscious, on his way to oblivion.

Eleanor has given me two medical books to read to learn
how to relax. It seems to be a science. I grow tense with the
effort of understanding, muscles tight, mind straining at the
professional jargon. No wonder I never mastered the trick.
Bertrand Russell once told me he taught himself to relax at
near eighty. "You go limp all over. Watch me," he said. We
were riding in the back seat of a car together in London, and
I felt his body collapse gently against mine. "Is your mind
limp?" I said.
"Not when I look at you."
He told B. and me we were the only Americans he had met
with whom he could relax. "Americans treat a man as if he
were a monument, or a public meeting."

M A R C H .   Henry Adams ended a bad-tempered letter to
his brother: "Forgive me if I seem irritated. Actually, I am
a great deal more irritated than I seem." These are remarks
to leave unsaid, unwritten, not jabbed on the page in capital
letters as I read themes at midnight and the students all appear
to be writing like Sweeney:

> I gotta use words when I talk to you
> But if you understand or if you dont
> That's nothing to me and nothing to you

Who is Henry Adams to educate, to teach one compassion?—
a cynic who said, as World War I began, "To me the crumbling
of worlds is always fun." (Henry Miller later echoed him:
"I am dazzled by the glorious collapse of the world.")

Tonight with the weather news, the cheery man who
announces the "finer Carolina weather" promised a tornado
before 11:00 P.M. "Thanks for intimidating me," I told him. The
sky shook with black clouds, tornadic winds, and approaching
funnels. A pine tree crashed in my woods. I thought of sitting

it out alone midst flying trees, then telephoned the Easleys:
"May I come over?" Cordially they invited me, to die with
them if necessary. They have a roomy basement for awaiting
tornadoes, hurricanes, or the end of the planet. I stayed the
night in their guest room, shamed by a mizzle rain with no
wind. Next morning the newspaper reported *four* tornadoes
wildly chasing over the state. I was a coward on instinct.

BAROMETERS

A straw in the wind is enough
To prophesy the gale,
Augur the pelting storm.
But for a reed more hollow,
Slenderer, more frail,
Pliant to bend, portend
The tornadic winds to follow
That you never foresaw—
Try a man of straw.

A P R I L .   After reading Auden and Hart Crane among
other poets this term, a student with much on his fretful mind
came to my office to talk and brought up the question of the
homosexual writer. Didn't a man write better if he was one?
Weren't the best authors—poets, novelists, playwrights—
homosexual? Didn't Freud say the artist is a misfit?

My, my, I thought, leaning back in my chair. What's the
answer to *that?* I said: well, you might defend the idea that
impotent husbands make the best writers by compiling a list
of famous men who didn't consummate their marriage: Swift,
Ruskin, Carlyle, Barrie, George Bernard Shaw, and so on. Or
you might offer impressive proof that the only successful poets
among women are unloved spinsters and recluses, naming
(offhand) Emily Brontë, Emily Dickinson, Christina Rossetti,
Edith Sitwell, Marianne Moore. You might conclude by a
tactful choice of examples that normal sexual behavior and a

happy marriage are ruinous to good writing. The artist is a misfit, said Freud. An eccentric, anyway.

But easiest to show, by the longest list of names, is that many a writer has had a consuming love affair with himself.

Edmond de Goncourt tells in the *Journals* of a dinner at the Café Riche with Flaubert, Zola, Turgenev, and Daudet: "We began with a long discussion on the special aptitudes of writers suffering from constipation and diarrhea . . ."

Flaubert and Goncourt also believed in celibacy as essential to an artist.

M A Y . People begin to read *Charley Smith's Girl*, now in print but not to be published till June, for which heaven help me. Either it is contradictory by nature or everyone reads it differently. The librarians think it is about books and a Reader. Some people find it grim, some funny, happy or unhappy, glad or despairing. Florence Blakely said it transmits fierce joy. "You *were* lucky, weren't you?" Marian Scott said it's a testimonial to why not to commit suicide.

Helen Brown wrote: "Please tell me why you are a successful mother-teacher-writer rather than a parolee of a detention home or psychiatric ward?"

Some quite rightly dislike it, too confessional; it jars them, offends, makes them uneasy. They avoid me, then say with marked constraint, "It would make a good movie, a period piece." Or, "Let me tell you sometime about my own childhood."

My beloved eighth-grade teacher, Miss Teresa Tanner, wrote with her wonderful inversions: "Glad am I that I did not know the truth when you were my pupil. Sorry am I that I did not know your mother, but confident am I that you, her daughter, brought her joy. Very grateful am I that you remembered me."

And she taught me English.

On the other hand, Ned Knowles complains that I didn't put enough sex play into my story. "You must have suppressed it,"

he says. "Sex happens to everybody." Dear me, I told about
my Uncle Horton's attempt to rape me, didn't I? But that was
not play. I'm sorry now I forgot to include the erotic scene
when I was five and my playmate Manley showed me his
garter.

I was fifteen when my dentist fell in love with me, an old
married man of thirty-five whose first move towards seduction
was to lend me Krafft-Ebing, which I dutifully smuggled into
the house and read. It was clear he hadn't read it himself, since
he only tried to kiss me with trembling lips. The discomfort
of this performance was that, each time I opened my mouth
wide the way you do in a dental chair, I couldn't tell whether
his intention was to use the drill on my rear molars or plant a
kiss. This weakened my rapport with dentists. Years later when
one of them snarled, "Wipe that lipstick off your mouth!" I
thought, "The old lecher, *now* what is he going to do?"

I think a great deal about the way the book ends, "There
must be a third way." I worry about that, the third way—not
my mother Lizzie's, which was endurance to the end of her
life, loneliness, fortitude; not my father Charley's, which was
giving up in despair and turning his face to the wall, saying
not a word till he died. I know very well what the third way
is, the courage to be happy. The obligation not to be unhappy.
Only I can't find it.

Virginia Woolf found the publishing of a book a fearful
ordeal (and she had her own Hogarth Press, with her husband
as publisher and no rejection slips). Her friends hurt her most.
Their loud silence was cruel and, it seemed to her, calculated.
Of *A Room of One's Own*, she wrote, "It occurs to me how
I'm disliked, how I'm laughed at; and I'm rather proud of my
intention to take the fence gallantly." Of *Three Guineas*, she
wailed in her diary, "My own friends have sent me to
Coventry over it." And again, "Not one of my friends has
mentioned it."

My friends, on the whole, make a lovely fuss. The others?
The words they do *not* speak, their evasions, to quote Mrs.
Gamp, "lambs could not forgive . . . nor worms forget."

And now, kind friends, what I have wrote
I hope you will pass o'er,
And not criticize as some have done
Hitherto herebefore.

—Julia A. Moore, the Sweet Singer of Michigan

"But for women, I thought, looking at the empty shelves, these difficulties are infinitely more formidable." —*A Room of One's Own*

J U N E .   David is here with his family, now that the college term is over for us both. Last night, to surprise the little boys, three and two years old, he blew lungfuls of air into an enormous inflatable rubber giraffe, tall as himself, and placed it outside their bedroom to greet them first thing this morning. In the night Stephen woke and opened his door. There he saw looming up before him what appeared to be a real live giraffe, outlined by the light of the moon. He crept back into his bed, covered his head with the blanket not to hear it galloping about, and wept.

In the morning, quick to remember, he woke Pip in the next bed. "Go and see if there's a giraffe out there." Pip rose obediently, opened the door, and went forth to look for a giraffe. He came back to report the good news.

"Yep, it's still there," he said.

CHILDREN ON A DUSTY ROAD

Steve, Pip, Kate, all three (aged one, two, and three)
Came down the road where the mockingbirds sing,
Listening, noticing.

"I want a tail," said Steve, "so I can be a mouse."
    "I want to fly,"
Said Pip, like Icarus in the sun.
Kate said nothing (aged one).

"I'll be Noah, so you be dead. No, you be God, Pip,"
   Stephen said.
"I is God," said Pip. But Kate
(Aged one) was only Kate.

J U L Y .   On a trip to California with Howard and Eleanor
in their airconditioned Plymouth (cold beer on ice in the picnic
hamper), I was alarmed to see how much Dante country we've
got in America—how much hell, I mean, as part of the
landscape.

It wasn't noticeable as far west as Ohio, a state I respect (I
married a man from Ohio) with its Super Duper markets, its
windowboxes of petunias in Upper Sandusky, its "Christ for
Van Wert, Ohio, Crusade." Indiana lay green and gold in the
sun with acres of soy beans on one side of the road, golden
oats on the other. Wisconsin was full of cows and cheddar
cheese, Minnesota of black turkeys, Brahmin cattle, and
windmills. A gopher crossed the road in Minnesota.

But by South Dakota things began to deteriorate, to look
sinister the moment we toured our first national monument.
Hell, it appeared, was under government management, a
tourist attraction free of charge, a scenic resort. Like Dante,
we were turned into hellgazers. As extinguishers of hope, the
Badlands of South Dakota were *bad*—170 miles of damnation,
where the sterile earth seemed carved by a madman into
outlandish pinnacles, weird turrets, spires, gorges. In that
tortured landscape without water, hostile to life, scarred with
cracks and fissures as if ready to crumble into dust, even my
thoughts were evil. Steinbeck called the Badlands the work of
an evil child. He was wrong. Satan did it, the devil himself
("I am a feend: my dwelling is in helle").

Tourists visit the Badlands by moonlight, actually do. They
come like the armies of sinners, equipped with picnic baskets
and strong nerves to camp overnight. They wait in line in the
museum to sign the visitors' book. "Wonderful!" they write.
"Proud to be an American." Nobody says, "*Lasciate ogni*

speranza, voi ch'entrate!" Nobody laments, "Why this is hell,
nor am I out of it."

The town of Dante, South Dakota, was appropriately named.
Go-to-Hell Gulch, S.D., had much the same ring. You saw what
they meant by the signboards on the highway: "If you lived
here, you'd be home now." And "Come as you are."

It's a great pity Walt Whitman never identified America as
Dante country. He might have written an Inferno, a whole
Divine Comedy, instead of yawping the "Song of Myself" ("I
dote on myself, there is that lot of me and all so luscious").
Though the lot of him was the size of the U.S.A. from coast to
coast, he never traveled west of the Mississippi.

At Yellowstone National Park, we received a litter bag and
a warning about bears: "Report any bear damage" (which I
took to mean damage from the bears, not any harm we might
do them). The stench of sulphur rose ominously (as it did in
the sixth circle of Hell, where Dante was assailed by a disgust-
ing stench so powerful he was paralyzed by the fumes). The
earth shook. Scalding water roared from two hundred erupting
geysers, ten thousand boiling springs, steaming hellholes, pools
red as blood. (In the seventh circle of Hell, Dante saw a river
of boiling blood, brimful of sinners.) These infernal waters at
Yellowstone spewed forth, squirted, hissed, sputtered, threatened, moaned "Like sighs, lamentations, and loud wailings."
Bubbling hot mud went plop, plop in a fearsome fashion like
the bubbles from the fourth circle of Hell, made by the gurgling souls of the Slothful drowning in slime and muck. Their
sighs of despair caused the bubbles to heave. And Dante and
Virgil made a wide arc around them with eyes fixed in horror
on the gulping, gobbling mud. We too walked with fear in
our hearts, slithering lost souls in the blinding mists, while
below our feet came tumult and bluster, mutterings from the
bowels of the earth. "Nature gone nuts," said Steinbeck. Nature
gone to hell.

As we entered the Craters of the Moon, Idaho, some 75
square miles of it, the ranger at the gate called out, "Have a
nice time!" The sky was black, spitting rain. Eating a box of
raisins to keep up our courage, we drove straight into hellfire
and brimstone. The earth writhed, the air trembled. Godless-

ness reigned. "Flee from folly on every side," sang Howard, "Here on the hills of Haversham." Stark cinder cones rose up like piles of coal tossed in the air, blobs and chunks of black lava. A chipmunk fled before us and I thought: that's odd, Dante said nothing of chipmunks in hell. This was once a cauldron.

After following the winding road for miles through its concentric circles, the three of us got gingerly out of the car to climb around the craters. From the rim of the Big Cone (Dante's Hell was a cone), fiery rivers of lava had flowed to cover the ruined valley. We struggled to the top, then leaned over the brim to peer into the abyss, the abode of the damned, the inferno of the ungodly. Hellgazers.

"I've got a raisin seed stuck in my tooth," said Howard.

So Dante may have remarked to Virgil as they looked, rueful and appalled, into the bottomless pit. Virgil was a wraith, a shade. But Dante walked in the human body, burdened by the suffering flesh.

In the end, however, one had to admit that the worst hell is not the devil's but my own, earthbound, manmade. Man is the culprit, contriver of his own hell, inhabiter of it. At Donner Memorial Park, Nevada, this plain truth darkened the mind. A wagon party of ninety emigrants, the Donner Party, started out in April, 1846, from Springfield, Illinois, on their way to California. They left the main migration and mostly on foot tried to take a cutoff from Great Salt Lake. The fate they met still numbs, still horrifies. Like Dante, one retreats in terror: "I had not thought death had undone so many."

Blocked by snows in the Sierra Nevada Mountains, trapped by winter from November to April, the desperate group camped and died in the frigid cold at Donner Lake, now one of our most popular national monuments and picnic areas (for boldhearts having the temerity to *eat* there). Half of them died of starvation or perished from attempts to escape over the mountain pass in the snow. Today the tourists bring their own beer and sandwiches. Something about the place whets the appetite. Certainly hell is full of happy tourists.

Donner Pass—cannibal pass. Those who survived proved in their lust for life demonic. They were men, they became cannibals—one Louis Kiesburg in particular, who ate human flesh and thrived. Of the 44 children along, seventeen of them were not yet six. Children of this company were killed and devoured.

In Canto XXXII, in the ninth circle of Hell, Dante witnessed such a gruesome meal. On an immense lake he saw two heads frozen together in one hole, the mouth of one gnawing with relish at the brain of the other. Then,

> Lifting his mouth from his horrendous meal,
> this sinner first wiped off his messy lips
> in the hair remaining on the chewed-up skull.

A few miles outside Reno, Nevada, as you leave the city of gamblers, girls, and wedding bells for divorcés, where the billboards say, "Let Yourself Go in Reno," a sign points to a pretty little country town just off the superhighway. HAPPY VALLEY, it says.

In a state like Nevada with no speed laws, you hardly have time to slow down to read the sign, let alone stop off for refreshment and ease of spirit. Yet how inviting it sounds—a green refuge, a village full of happy people, a garden in the desert, an anchorage, a haven of peace. It sounds like Eliot's still center. Like the promised land in a world where you live at your own risk. Like (as D. H. Lawrence said) "the ultima, ultima, ultima Thule."

Forget it. Forget the whole thing, take it off your mind and keep on going. No welcome at the end of the road awaits you there, no solution to life's sorrows. They probably won't let you in.

HAPPY VALLEY, the sign says. And underneath in small letters, "No services available."

I remember nothing of Phillipsburg, Kansas (which seems a shame since Kansas is the geographical center of the United States). On arrival at our motel Sunday afternoon, Howard made a proposal: if Eleanor and I would take a sleeping pill with our cocktails before dinner, we might be reasonably wide

awake next morning, ready for an early start on the home-
ward journey. It sounded forehanded to me to prepare at
5:00 P.M. for a good night's sleep, but Eleanor the doctor
agreed to the wisdom of it and got out her medical kit. She
holds the theory that a sleeping pill is most effective if taken
on an empty stomach. To be on the safe side, she administered
two apiece.

The cocktail hour was joyous, and in fine fettle we drove
off to a restaurant where I recall expressing my opinions with
some force over the roast beef, denouncing the picaresque
novel, I think it was. Not till the dessert did sleep overtake me
and my head fell into a dish of raspberry jello and whipped
cream. When Eleanor passed out at the same time, splashing
into her cup of coffee, two startled waitresses ran to our table
to see what was up.

"They aren't drunk," Howard explained. "They're drugged."

Refusing assistance from manager or patrons, he pulled us
to our feet and, grappling with one on either side, dragged us
unconscious to the door and out to the car. There, in trying to
unlock the door of the car with one hand and prop us against
it with the other, he lost his grip and let go. I went down flat
on my face in the gutter and Eleanor landed square on top
of me. I remember being roused by the jolt, just before I went
back to sleep. Expecting any moment to hear a police whistle,
Howard yanked and pushed to untangle us; then while the
waitresses watched and somebody cheered, he picked us up,
one body at a time like a gunny sack, threw us into the car,
and drove rapidly away.

AUGUST .   Poor Richard. I've never read *Poor Richards
Almanack* before. Now it's too late. I find him pretty rude and
homespun, the moral stargazer. If he had to borrow his
proverbs, maxims, adages, admonitions, saws, mottoes, apo-
phthegms, sayings, why did he change the words? A man who
kept an almanac for twenty-five years might well be hard up
for copy. But the old adage:

> Wikked tunge breketh bone
> Though the tunges self hath none

becomes

> Man's tongue is soft, and bone doth lack;
> Yet a stroke therewith may break a man's back.

How can a tongue break a man's back? At a stroke, too.

Ovid's beautiful *Ut amoris amabilis esto,* "If you would be loved, be lovable" (or as Moschus said before him: "Be kind to love, that he be kind to you"), is appropriated by B. Franklin to "If you would be beloved, make yourself amiable." A fig for that.

He paraphrased Shakespeare, in *III Henry VI,*

> And many strokes, though with a little axe,
> Hew down and fell the hardest-timber'd oak,

which is better poetry than Poor Richard's

> Little strokes fell great oaks.

He quoted Montaigne, who said: "It is no use thinking to leave one's humanity behind, for if we walk on stilts we still have to walk on our legs, and there is no way of sitting on the most elevated throne save on the bottom." Montaigne's word was *cul,* which means backside, I guess, or rump. Franklin said: "The greatest monarch on the proudest throne is oblig'd to sit upon his own arse." To mention a monarch's arse is Franklin's privilege, but it seems a bit vulgar; as a king sits so sits a god. In English, bottom is more polite.

And Montaigne said, "Nothing noble is done without risk" (*"Rien de noble se fait sans hasard"*). Cautious Richard weakened it into complacence: "The way to be safe is never to be secure." What ailed the man?

He was no poet. He had a tin ear. Matthew Arnold agreed. In the essay "Sweetness and Light," Arnold praised Franklin for his "imperturbable commonsense," and to prove that commonsense is not enough quoted a sample of a projected revised version of the Book of Job (which, according to Franklin, was obsolete in the King James Version). It would replace this passage: "Then Satan answered the Lord and said, 'Doth Job fear God for nought?'"

Franklin made his own translation: "Does your Majesty imagine that Job's good conduct is the effect of mere personal attachment and affection?" Even Satan never talked rot like that.

Poor Richard. He should have copied into his almanac, from the Bible of King James, "The ear trieth words as the mouth tasteth meat."

SEPTEMBER.　　Three years ago the Duke students listened to a three-day panel on "The Post-Christian Man." Last year it was "The Post-Human Man" with Poet Snodgrass. This year it is "The Post-Moral Man." Maybe the latest model is all three at once. That's what I said when a student asked me to meet with the organizers to discuss what presumably they have got themselves into this time when the theologians come, "plus a writer I forget who," the student said. I said I would be no help, since I was an old-fashioned moralist, *ante*, not *post*, then hastily spelled out the joke for fear he was hearing it *anti*.

The writer is Lawrence Lipton, Professor of Avant-Garde Studies at U.C.L.A., author of *The Erotic Revolution*, in which he "makes a strong case for a new morality." Poor old morality.

I agree with Galileo that the world does move.

"There are some people who wear the same face for years; naturally it wears out, it gets dirty, it splits at the folds, it stretches, like gloves one has worn on a journey. . . . Other people put their faces on, one after the other, with uncanny rapidity and wear them out."
　　　　　—Rilke, *The Notebooks of Malte Laurids Brigge*
You can't win either way. The face just wears out.

David sent me a fine line from a sixteenth-century morality play: "But soft, the royal hinges squeak."

F. L. Lucas writes in an essay "On Books": "From six to eleven I was allowed to run loose in a library. It was a tiny example of free enterprise; and the wastefulness of free enterprise may be a small price to pay for independence. Ever since, I have felt a passionate contempt—perhaps excessive—for people who want to be taught, instead of teaching themselves; for the packs of little jackals that run yelping together in literary movements or critical cliques; for all who cannot walk alone in the isolation of totally unpopular opinions, with the disdainful aloofness of cats."

Mr. Lucas teaches at the University of Cambridge. I give him credit for unintentional irony. As teacher he can't afford to be disdainful and aloof (but is on the contrary, I've heard, a kind and patient man). Besides, the ability to walk alone should fill him with lofty thoughts, free of contempt for the crowds of hollow men who lean and hang together. It should rid him of scorn, an ugly thing; of mockery, which is unseemly. In this savage outburst, he vents his rage and may feel better for it. But why as a cat who walks by himself should he be out hunting jackals?

Somewhere in his delightful books F. L. Lucas defines happiness, its causes and conditions. One of them, I remember, is a calmly balanced imperturbability. Another is the ability to accept the inevitable. A little stupidity in the world, as Mr. Lucas is well aware, is inevitable.

Yeats said a splendid thing about his father and the Dublin mob (whose violence at the Abbey Theatre stopped the performance of *The Playboy of the Western World*): "I fought them, he was nobler—he forgot them."

OCTOBER. Betty Ropp and I went to see "The Knack," a wacky English film meaning the knack of taking a girl to bed. A tremendous bed played expertly the main role, and the young lovers looked like London these days, not very appetizing.

By going to a movie once or twice a year, I witness the

revelation of sex and the socalled private parts. Adam has finally lost his fig-leaf, life its asterisks. What happens if you go twice a week?

The "Today" television show appears at 7:00 A.M., a time when I do not seek entertainment. I've never watched it, but today I didn't need to. A hundred other people did and told me so, plus two friends in New York who made hurried long-distance calls. Such is fame on television. Mr. Downs read on his show a list of odd and funny graffiti he had collected. One of them, found scrawled on the wall of a Greenwich Village bar, said, "Helen Bevington is a neo-classical fink."

One listener heard it as "fake," which spoils the poetry.

The New School for Social Research in New York offers a course in graffiti, the art of writing on walls. (B. used to recite a couplet: "A man's ambition must be small / To write his name on a shithouse wall.") I'll bet this one about me was written by a graduate of that school.

> Somtyme to sober, somtyme to sadde,
> Somtyme to mery, somtyme to madde,
> Somtyme I syt as I were solemke prowde;
> Somtyme I laughe ouer loude.
>
> —Skelton, *Magnificence*

John Skelton called a girl a pode in "Manerly Margery Mylk and Ale":

> By Gad, ye be a pretty pode,
> And I love you an hole cartlode.

I asked three professors of medieval language and literature what a *pode* is. One thought it an indecent word for pudendum. Another guessed it meant a pea pod. The third said he didn't know. I spent a brief time with dictionaries and found it means toad. (In the Middle Ages, toads and frogs were "podys" and "froskys.")

Dr. Johnson playfully labeled Fanny Burney a toad. On discovering her to be the author of *Evelina*, "Oh, she's a toad!"

he cried, "a sly young rogue! with her Smiths and her Branghtons!"

Phryne means *toad* in Greek, a name given to courtesans.

Alison, the young wife in the "Miller's Tale," looked like a weasel:

> Fair was this yonge wyf, and therwithal
> As any wesele hir body gent and smal.

John Crowe Ransom wrote a poem about a pigeon, "Husband Betrayed," and a man who loved her. He gave his girl the pet name "Pigeon" and married her, only to discover she was indeed pigeonwitted (and pigeontoed?). He had wived a bird:

> And so he called her Pigeon,
> Saying to himself, "She flutters walking
> And in sweet monotone she twitters talking."
> Nothing was said of her religion.

She had a snowy bosom, pecked her food, preened herself— when what he wanted was a woman, "To sit and drudge and serve him as was common."

But a pigeon is a dove, a dove is a pigeon and lacks gall— the same bird, if only poets knew it. Call a girl a dove and she will love you. ("Open to me, my sister, my love, my dove, my undefiled.") And a dove she remains to the end. (Paulina, in *Winter's Tale:* "I an old turtle / Will wing me to some withered bough.")

Or please her with endearment by calling her a mouse, not mousy. (Only a man is a rat.)

> "God bless you, mouse," the bridegroom said,
>   And smakt her on the lips." —Warner, *Albion's England*

> "Good my mouse of virtue, answer me." —*Twelfth Night*

La Fontaine wrote a charming fable, "Mouse into Maiden."

A feminine rhyme from *The Proverbs of John Heywood:*

> But pryde she sheweth none, her look reason alloweth,
> She looketh as butter would not melt in her mouth.

NOVEMBER.   David made a jack-o-lantern for the children out of one of Howard Easley's huge yellow pumpkins. At Stephen's request it was carved with the mask of tragedy on one side, comedy on the other. What a literary child. We viewed it dispassionately from both sides, running around the table where it sat, a two-faced Janus, laughing and weeping.

Now they have gone home to Charlottesville, and the jack-o-lantern, lying on the compost heap, has wrinkled and dwindled into the November of old age. The comic mask has become gradually a tragic one, with drooping, turned-down mouth. This is what happens to a laughing face?

When the Pattons came tonight (with my family departed), we tried to think of the social talents a child should be taught for future need and grace. To learn French, we agreed. To swim. To dance. To listen. To forgive. To grow flowers. To ride a horse. To solfegge, I said. "What in the world is that?" asked Fanny, disapproving. "I'm sure I never learned that in the South."

To love. When I was young—at least by the time I got to college—we had free verse and free love. They were the curriculum, though I wasn't good at either one. They lacked rules, purely arbitrary as to length of line and length of duration. It was a distinct relief to me when T. S. Eliot declared himself against free verse, saying there was no such thing, a "preposterous fiction." When verse becomes free, it stops being verse. The same thing I found to be true of love: it wasn't free either. Each, you might say, tends to lose its melodic line. Each is a misnomer, costing, Eliot would agree, not less than everything.

But in my day, freedom in love or verse meant rebellion, escape from conformity. Now it means conformity, following the fashion. To rebel—does one want the child to rebel? Or merely to be loving and giving.

DECEMBER.   I turn on the radio for the sound of human voices, or the television for the shape of human beings. I stand looking at Howard's cows in the meadow because they are moving, unruffled and alive; at a yellow cat crossing the dooryard. I like the sound of a fly buzzing at the window, or a bird hopping across the porch roof as if walking on dry toast.

That is loneliness.

1966

JANUARY.   Tonight the Easleys and I gave a whopper of a New Year's Eve party, at which the hostesses Eleanor and I displayed more endurance and joy than our guests. We danced, carrying off the men since at our age we can't waste time waiting to be asked. Dancing is love and laughter, so why are men so quick to give it up? After midnight supper and kisses all round, Eleanor cried, "Let's have the Beer Barrel Polka!" and put on another record. I loved dancing with David, the best dancer on the floor (like my father Charley, but not tipsy). These snatched moments make up for the lost nights, these incredible shifts to happiness, the alternation of dark and light.

Someone said with utter sweetness, "Helen wears out all the men."

The girl who shampoos my hair nearly killed herself this morning while driving to work. She swerved to miss a tiny gray squirrel, flipped completely over in her little Renault, demolished the brand new car, barely escaped with her life. But she missed the squirrel.

Each weekend her husband goes out to shoot squirrels for sport. Tonight she must tell him what happened. Tears fill her eyes. She trembles and takes another tranquilizer.

"For a *squirrel?*" he will say. "You fool. You crazy fool!"

St. Francis of Assisi wore bells around his ankles to warn the crickets out of the way to avoid stepping on them.

When things go wrong in Rosa's life and her head is blouzed up with trouble (as when her car was stolen last Saturday night), she takes some jolt medicine. She won't tell me the name of it.

Rosa has a got-rights cat. It has got rights the same as everybody. I have a lot of vocabulary to learn from Rosa.

FEBRUARY.   David startled me by saying with calm indifference, no, he was not a Socialist. I don't know why I asked; we never talk about politics. I must have assumed that one is, that I am, which dates me indeed, like being a Mugwump. I think I'm a Socialist, whatever in this hapless world the word means. It has become obsolete in this country, finished, a visionary dream if not a disreputable one. To David it has no meaning, thirty years having passed since it was a democratic idea of equality in the American air. It seemed to B. and me a plan of fair distribution.

I asked Stephen Spender a while ago if he was a Socialist. "Yes, I suppose I am," he said. "Yes."

Francis Brown published my essay on T. S. Eliot and the way to Little Gidding in "Speaking of Books," page two of the New York *Times Book Review*. People not only read that page but are prompted to write the author long chatty letters. If there is peace to be found at Little Gidding, they want clearer directions, more particulars. And a map. One letter came from a soldier stationed near Little Gidding, who married a girl there and has never heard of Eliot. Another brought love from a descendant of the Ferrars, who started the religious community of Little Gidding in 1626. Her mother's name was Mary Ferrar. She is eighty-two, unmarried, the grandmother of seven children, having adopted two little girls long ago. She moved from England to the village of Alfred, New York, a religious community eight miles from my hometown. She brought Little Gidding with her, and I wish I might have found it there.

MARCH.   T. S. Eliot wrote in "Ash Wednesday" that in order to rejoice one must construct something upon which to rejoice. He then constructed the Eliot retirement home, the "Shantih" with its rose garden, and rejoiced in the peace that is God. I see that Paul Valéry, a great egoist, did a bit of constructing (or salvation-seeking) too: "By dint of constructing . . . I truly believe that I have constructed myself." Rejoice, rejoice.

Ten years ago I cut out a picture from *Time* of what looked to be a prizefighter in the ring, raising his arm in victory, his opponent out of sight flat on the floor. It was T. S. Eliot delivering a lecture on poetry in a sports stadium in Minneapolis to 13,727 intent listeners. At least they seemed spellbound, a beautiful thing to see.

Yesterday I read a piece about Eliot by Stephen Spender who refers to this performance in Minnesota. He quotes Eliot: "I felt like a very small bull walking into an enormous arena." (A bull six feet tall in formal attire?) But Spender says there were 13,523 present, casually dropping two hundred and four spectators. That's too many for a poet to lose.

David and Peggy gave me a Vermeer for the kitchen. It is brimful of placidity. The tranquil seventeenth-century lady in white starched collar and cap standing at her window calms my mind. Her house is ordered, her world is still. Vermeer must have known peace in Delft to paint interiors full of sunlight and women so gentle. I cook an egg at the stove and bask in her sweet content.

Howard came into the kitchen, took one disgusted look, and said, "What is that damned nun doing on your wall?"

I said, "That's not a nun. That's a housewife."

My seminar in modern poetry had a surprise party for me. When I came into the classroom this afternoon, the twelve were sitting around a table strewn with paper plates of potato chips and chocolate cookies. Sherry was served in beer mugs and paper cups. To make the scene thoroughly disorderly, they had brought two electric guitars, everything but party hats and confetti.

A while ago when we read Auden's silly ballad "Miss Gee,"

about a poor unloved spinster who, denied a child in her womb, produces a cancer there and dies of it,

> Let me tell you a little story
> About Miss Edith Gee;
> She lived in Clevedon Terrace
> At Number 83,

I said I had never heard of the "St James Infirmary Blues" to which the grisly tale is supposed to be sung. And a naked confession that was. The class shuddered at such illiteracy—not know the great jazz number performed by Lead Belly himself? I know it now. At the party all twelve sang all 23 stanzas at the top of their lungs to the accompaniment of two guitars. Nobody came and threw us out of the building. A lovely party.

APRIL.   While I waited at the Raleigh-Durham airport for a friend's plane to arrive, I listened to a boy in uniform, no more than eighteen, on his way to fight in Vietnam. He was brimful of bravado, talking in a shrill, scared voice to a Negro in uniform sitting beside him.

"When I get over there, man," he said, leaping to his feet, "when I get over to that goddam Vietnam and I see anything moving, y'know, man, I'll kill him! Like this, man. K-k-k-k-k-k. Boy, I'm telling you, I mean like wow! man. He makes a move. K-k-k-k-k-k. He's *dead!*"

Steve and Pip are asking for another baby. "Why are all our eggs not hatching?" Stephen asks with a touch of impatience. "We need a new baby. It could be a boy and we could call him Laura."

Anacreon was a lascivious and intemperate poet, says Lemprière, much given to wine-bibbing. Yet he achieved honor and longevity, surviving to his eighty-fifth year. When he came to die, it was by choking to death, says Pliny, on a grape.

Anacreon sang the happy songs of a reveler, praising love
and wine. He sounds squiffy, but Athenaeus declares whatever the rumor he was not. Being an upright man, says
Athenaeus, he stayed sober and only pretended to be drunk.

One thirst-quenching verse of Anacreon's is about the earth,
trees, oceans, rivers, sun, all drinking up the rain. As for
himself,

> Am I the one
> Lone thing on earth
> That's always dry?
> Not I, my friends,
> Not I.

I believe Anacreon drank enough wine to avoid the charge
of sobriety, like the Chinese poet, Li Po, who lived in the
time of, but not to age of, the Venerable Bede. (The Venerable
Bede died at 62.) "Drunken I rose and walked to the moonlit
stream," wrote Li Po. He died of reaching out to embrace the
moon in the water.

Robert Herrick, who loved Anacreon and imitated him in
his Anacreontics (in praise of the girls, the wine, the song),
gave him full credit for taking a couple of drinks too many.
In "The Vision," Herrick says,

> Methought I saw (as I did dream in bed)
> A crawling vine about Anacreon's head:
> Flushed was his face; his hairs with oil did shine;
> And as he spake, his mouth ran o'er with wine.
> Tippled he was; and tippling lisped withall;
> And lisping reeled, and reeling like to fall.
> A young Enchantress close by him did stand
> Tapping his plump thighs with a myrtle wand:
> She smiled; he kissed; and kissing, culled her too;
> And being cup-shot, more he could not do.
> For which (methought) in pretty anger she
> Snatched off his crown, and gave the wreath to me:
> Since when (methinks) my brains about do swim,
> And I am wild and wanton like to him.

———

POET OF THE GRAPE

Anacreon sang of love and wine:
The lady and the laden vine
Were tune to him and anodyne.

And thus, within an arbor shady,
His light Anacreontics made he
To praise the luster of his lady,

Her glow, her ripe and rounded shape,
The tendrils curling at the nape—
And died of choking on a grape.

I had assumed the Venerable Bede lived to be at least 150. At the end of his *Ecclesiastical History*, he said of life at Jarrow, "I took sweet pleasure in always learning, teaching, or writing"—the way, you would think, to live forever. But he died of mortal fevers at 62, after distributing his possessions (a little pepper, a little incense). He sat on the floor of his cell chanting "Glory be to the Father and to the Son and to the Holy Ghost," and died, while the angels sang "Amen, Venerable Bede."

Dante put the Venerable Bede in Paradise (X,130), quite a compliment since he was the only Englishman Dante allowed inside.

MAY.   Which do the young elect to follow, the hellgazers or the rejoicers? Heaven over hell every time. I've read so many term papers endorsing Dylan Thomas and his version of life in *Under Milk Wood* ("Oh, isn't life a terrible thing, thank God!") that it seems every girl fancies herself the town prostitute Polly Garter and every boy wants to sleep with her, "Under the Milkwood tree, / Who loves to lie with me." Should I send them next to Thomas Dekker?

'What's your name, I pray?"
"Penelope Whorehound. I come of the Whorehounds."
                              —*The Honest Whore*

As I drove to the University this morning, thinking about
Richard Wilbur whose poetry we would read in class, saying
over a line of his, "It is by words and the defeat of words—" I
made a sudden resolution, at the stoplight at Broad and Club
Boulevard, to unlearn my words.

I will stop using the word *lonely*. I will change it to
independent or *alone*. Aloneness is not the same thing as
loneliness. I will live an independent life, fraught with
freedom. I will stop explaining my plight to myself, using
charged words like *fear*, like *grief*. It is not only cowardly but
Byronic (Byron: "I learned to love despair"). By the defeat of
words I grieve. It is myself I mourn for.

Richard Wilbur says, "The subjects to which a poet returns
are those which vex him." This proves me no poet: I return
to such things as love and birdsong. I have never written an
unhappy verse, thank God. Vexed, maybe, but only by my
words.

Words, words, words. Shakespeare could place three adjectives in a row and make them immortal. In *Macbeth:* "How
now, you secret, black, and midnight hags?" In *The Merchant
of Venice:* "Lean, rent, and beggared by the strumpet wind."
He could take three nouns and define misery: "These griefs,
these woes, these sorrows make me old" (Nurse in *Romeo
and Juliet*), or four nouns and define love (Lysander to
Hermia): "One heart, one bed, two bosoms, and one troth."
He could "Charm ache with air and agony with words."

Split is a versatile word. You can split hairs, straws, rails,
wood, votes, fees, infinitives, peas, the ears, the air, the atom,
the difference, the personality, a second, a banana, and your
sides with laughter.
"Blow, and split thyself," cried Shakespeare. "Let sorrow
split my heart."

———

Montaigne: "Words are made to follow and wait upon us.
I want my subject to capture and inflame the imagination of
my listener so that he will have no time to remember the
words. When I see a noble expression, I do not exclaim, 'It
is well said,' but 'It is well thought.'"

"What more do I know about a horse," he asked Fabrizio,
"when I am told that in Latin it is called *equus?*"
                    —Stendhal, *Charterhouse of Parma*

This is the real thing, I said rubbing my hands, a book of
talk: *The Oxford Book of English Talk.* I could hardly wait
to hear the 122 pieces in it—talk, talk, talk, from Margery
Kempe speaking aloud in 1417 to Mr. John Betjeman verbal-
izing in 1949.

Five and a half centuries ago, Margery Kempe, accused
of being a whore and a heretic, sounded like this when
examined by the Archbishop of York as to her faith:

At the last the seyd Erchebishchop cam into the Chapel wyth
hys clerkys, and sharply he seyde to hir, "Why gost thu in white?
Art thu a mayden?"

Sche, knelyng on hir knees befor hym, seyd, "Nay, ser, I am
no mayden: I am a wife."

Mr. John Betjeman, taking part in a proceedings to save the
little village of Letcombe Bassett from destruction, arguing
against Mr. Thomas Sharp who wanted to tear it down, ended
his oration like this:

"Steady on, Thomas. I know you don't want to pull everything
down any more than I do. Well, perhaps we'd better leave
Letcombe Bassett alone, hm?"

The 122 passages are very audible. Yet the editor and I
don't agree as to what makes talk worth listening to. Professor
James Sutherland records *how* people have spoken for centuries, not what they had to say. I expected talk that was a
dazzlement to the mind. What I heard was only a surprise
to the ear.

———

"Most of my neighbors speak the same language as I am writing here," said Montaigne. "But whether they think the same thoughts I cannot say."

J U N E . The Diary of Anaïs Nin is a sobering encounter with an obsession—herself. "My diary is my kief, hashish, and opium pipe. This is my drug and my vice"—her confessional and escape. It is not self-love; it is self-rapture. Even as a child of eleven she carried around a notebook in a little straw basket. Except for this first published volume, the diary exists in stacks of some 150 volumes in a bank vault in Brooklyn. That is what can happen if unchecked.

How does she sound? As longwinded as the *Decline and Fall*, the *Ring* cycle, or the wooing of Penelope; and humorless (one has to be humorless to go on like that). In a "natural flow," she writes her life moment by moment. "I feel no boundaries within myself, no walls, no fears. . . . I feel mobile, fluid." A reader's patience has boundaries.

E. B. White says a favorite book of his is a novel by Laurids Bruun, *Van Zanten's Happy Days*. Since my favorite book is anything Mr. White writes, I hurry to the library to share his delight.

Ball One for Mr. White. Every man to his own lotus eating, but he is wrong about *Van Zanten's Happy Days*. Aside from a good title, it lacks persuasion. Van Zanten went native in a simpleminded manner on a South Sea island among black savages, convinced that Eden still exists and he had returned to it in a bamboo hut. After finding unmixed joy in the arms of a female savage, with her fears, superstitions, indolence, and lusts, then losing her in a typhoon, he hated thereafter all white women, who by contrast appeared civilized.

Mr. White used to dream in print about Dorothy Lamour wearing only a sarong and a hibiscus flower, rising up from a swamp to welcome him to jungle madness. Or, as he said, to "amorous felicity."

JULY.   I invited Howard and Eleanor to see the film "Who's Afraid of Virginia Woolf?" It turned out to be a grotesque choice for their wedding anniversary! We witnessed this howling nightmare of unhappy marriage of a middleaged college professor and his bitchy wife. I've never seen a campus the likes of this one, or a faculty couple resembling these ferocious two; I profoundly hope that Howard (a middleaged professor) and Eleanor discovered no self-portrait in two childless people who devoured each other like cannibals. Eleanor and I sat captive, shivering, harrowed and numb. Howard said with undue gallantry it was the best picture he had ever slept through. Later he admitted he lied.

There was no catharsis in such goings on, no possible purgation. I wondered, as I have before, can a vicious story be written by a kind person? Demonstrably not. Edward Albee is culpable, a blameworthy man who hates women, including in her innocence Virginia Woolf. He should be stopped by public outrage from using her name without right or reason. What a vulgarity. What a callous world to allow it, to be amused.

One thing in favor of living in the country, it provides two excitements, daily anticipatory events—the weather and the mailman. Rain or shine, rather than lift my eyes to solicit a godsend from the preoccupied gods, I go and look in the mailbox for deliverance. Any belief is built on faith.

Now in 97° parching heat, I'm writing about life in the year 1937, whose summer temperature I don't recall. Temp. also passes.

AUGUST.   I've never seen a godwit. It is not a man, but a bird. It used to be thought good to eat when fattened. Ben Jonson ate the godwit. He invited his friends to partake at his table "Of partrich, pheasant, wood-cock . . . and *godwit*, if we can." Sir Thomas Browne called it the daintiest dish in England, the most costly too.

You can spot a godwit on our Carolina coast, they say, if

you are a birdwatcher on the lookout for snipes. Its bill curls upwards and it has pipestem legs. Whoever named it *godwit?* Nobody seems to know. Perhaps the bird named itself, out of pride, crying "Godwít, godwít."

THE GODWIT

There is the blacktailed godwit that shrieks and barks
And the bartailed godwit that breeds in Lapland.
With us the godwit is a migrant,
Unlike the meadowlarks.

Caliban called it a scamel on a rock,
Causing despair among Shakespearean critics,
Who glossed it as seagull, shellfish, seamew,
Or some kind of hawk.

An outwit is the godwit, in consequence.
But as to its being godlike or godwitted?
(At courting, say, a Zeus. In war, a Titan)
Lacking is evidence.

SEPTEMBER. A man told Picasso he didn't understand his paintings. Picasso asked, "Do you understand Chinese?" No, the man didn't. "It can be learned," said Picasso.

That may have silenced the man, but not me. Chinese can be learned as an orderly language, a discipline. I doubt that Picasso can, even by Picasso.

I finished my book today, two years after B.'s death. It began lonely and there is no end. It is about a love affair, mine, but Henry Simon will not find it sensational enough. My father Charley was a character, as Henry saw him, a wild old wicked man, a caution, whose life was enough to curl your hair. Henry loved Charley and Lizzie, regarding them as invented, fictional persons. Maybe I did too.

He will not find B. that kind of tumultuous hero. Out of

love I deprive B. of his dimensions, his true griefs and measures. I make him sound like a man who believed that whatever is, is right—a Deist, if ever you met one. That is unfair to B. He was wiser than that, more skeptical, in doubt, troubled by man's folly and indifferent to any god's. I have botched it again.

OCTOBER.   Mary Moorman, the biographer of Wordsworth, is the wife of the Bishop of Ripon. On her mother's side, she descends from Mrs. Humphry Ward, who was a niece of Matthew Arnold and an aunt of Aldous Huxley. On her father's side she claims Lord Macaulay and the two Trevelyans. And she spends her life writing a two-volume work on Wordsworth.

But tonight she talked at Duke to a handful of us about her illustrious family, "A Family of Letters," from notes she had scribbled into a threepenny notebook and, in an endearing and nervewracking performance, could barely read in her tiny script. She closed by reciting a stanza of Milton's "Nativity Ode." I think her aim was to show her agnostic father, G. M. Trevelyan (who read Milton to her as a child), not far removed in spirit from her Anglican husband. At the first line she broke down and wept. Only an amateur could have carried it off. It charmed.

I met the Moormans in London, at the Hotel Sandringham where we were both staying. She introduced herself at that time by saying simply, "I am Trevelyan's daughter." Tonight I fell in love with the Bishop, who filled me with beatitude. I took a shine to him (or from him). He is a small benign man, one of the pure in heart who appeal to me and plague me. The mystery is, was he born lovable and by accident became a churchman, or (I hate to believe) does his calling make him merry? I'm far from convinced that a man of peace has to be a man of God.

At a small party afterward, when he was asked to name his drink the Bishop said gently, "A martini, if you please," adding "on the rocks." At 11:00 P.M.? I sat immovable beside him, enveloped in blessedness, breathing in his saintly presence perfumed by juniper. Both Moormans are innocents, removed from this sinful world into Yorkshire, where they enjoy the old stately ways of England, Wordsworth, good works, Anglicans and ancestors. He is such a fine Bishop.

I have a passion for saints (being a witch myself of the order of Mother Damnable). Saints never have to be exorcised, extirpated, or arointed, though their actions, called miracles, are magical enough to shame the devil. Saints seem to attract miracles.

Take St. Denis: he was beheaded at Paris in 272 and departed from the block carrying his mitred head in his hands for the next six miles. According to Fraser's *Golden Bough,* there are *seven* heads of St. Denis collected and preserved in churches over Europe as relics of his extraordinary presence of mind. As is usual with sacred relics, I suppose a certificate of authenticity is hung nearby.

An Irish saint, St. Colman, who died in 611, had a trained housefly. Each day as the good man read his holy books, the devout fly would trot up and down the page to keep him company. If it happened that St. Colman was interrupted and called away from his cell, the fly would sit down upon the line where he had stopped reading and keep his place.

In the Roman Catholic church, says Laurence Housman, there are certain blessed saints who from the very day of their birth steadfastly refused the breast each Friday as an act of fasting and pious self-denial.

As for angels, there must be plenty of angels about, since angelologists are still at work studying them and their visitations. W. H. Auden notes that according to fourteenth-century cabalists, the total number of angels is 301,655,722. If it is true angels are immortal and do not multiply, or (Milton thought otherwise) even make love, the number must remain constant.

Yet Wallace Stevens, in his poem "Evening without Angels," asks why angels? Why seraphim with lutes and a coiffeur of haloes? "Was the sun concoct for angels or for men?" For men, he says. "Bare night is best. Bare earth is best. Bare, bare." No angels.

If not angels, why not houris in a Moslem Heaven (a heaven obviously created for men. Where do the women go?). Houris are the blackeyed damsels like gazelles, formed of pure musk and spices, made for love, who remain perpetual virgins to their lovers since their virginity is the kind that is renewable. Byron longed for that heaven,

> Secure in paradise to be
> By houris loved immortally.

NOVEMBER.   "The heart can begin again," said Colette. It can or it can't. Writers offer without stint these conflicting statements (what can and what can't be done), which sound equally well either way. "My mind to me a kingdom is," said Sir Edward Dyer. It is or (if you mean my mind) it isn't.

Montaigne found such arbitrariness good. He believed in the arbitrary choice, in diversity of opinion. One is free to think whatever gives him the most repose. "I offer [my opinions] as what I believe, not what is to be believed."

Writers agree or disagree. It doesn't matter, since either way makes sense. Some agree, for example, to praise work as the only reprieve:

Jules Renard: "I know only one truth. Work alone creates happiness. I am sure only of that one thing, and I forget it all the time."

John Steinbeck: "One is never drained by work but only by idleness. Lack of work is the most enervating thing in the world."

Virginia Woolf: "The only way I keep afloat is by working."

But not Faulkner, not he. William Faulkner considered it the saddest fact in life that the one thing a man can do for eight hours a day, day after day, is work. You can't eat eight

hours a day, or drink, or make love—all you can do for eight
hours is work. To Faulkner work is Adam's curse. To Philip
Larkin, as well:

> Why should I let the toad *work*
> squat on my life?
> Can't I use my wit as a pitchfork
> and drive the brute off?

Writers often seem to agree on the pleasure of forgetting:

Madame de Sévigné, to her daughter: "It is a pleasure, my
love, to have no memory at all."

Montaigne: "Memory is entirely lacking in me. To learn
three lines of poetry I need three hours."

Jules Renard: "I forget everything! It is wonderfully con-
venient."

Yet Richard Porson, the great classical scholar, couldn't
forget a thing and didn't try. He once offered to learn by
heart a copy of the London *Morning Chronicle*. After reading
a page or two from a book, he would close the book and
repeat it word for word. A student of his said, "Can the
Professor repeat it backwards?" This he did, missing two
words. As he poured forth from memory torrents of literature,
his charm was said (by some) to be irresistible.

His father's name was Huggin Porson. I like to remember
that.

Poets naturally disagree about poetry:

Yeats: "A poem comes right with a click like a closing box."

W. H. Auden: "A poem is never finished, it is only abandoned."

Most writers agree about sheep:

Sir Thomas More (in *Utopia*) exclaimed at the pride of a
man wearing fine wool, the same wool a sheep once wore,
"and yet was she all that time no other thing than a sheep."

In *Much Ado about Nothing*, when the violins play, Bene-
dict says, "Is it not strange that sheep's guts should hail
souls out of men's bodies?"

Dr. Johnson: "Sir, I am a better judge of mutton than any sheep."

But not about birdsong. The nightingale sang to Keats a "plaintive anthem," pouring forth its soul in ecstasy. T. S. Eliot recorded it as "'Jug Jug' to dirty ears," not quite agreeing with John Lyly:

> O 'tis the ravished nightingale,
> "Jug, jug, jug, jug, tereu," she cries,
> And still her woes at midnight rise.

William Cullen Bryant listened to the bobolink. "Spink spank spink," it sang, though Ornithologist Dawson says it really sounds like this: "Oh, geezeler, geezeler, gilipity, on-kcler, oozeler, oo."

Gerard Manley Hopkins heard the lark pour, pelt, spill its song like a skein of twine paid out from a tightly wound reel, "In crisps of curl off wild winch whirl." Shakespeare heard a blithe chant, "tirra-lirra."

The tit, said Gilbert White of Selborne, goes "tink, tink, tink." But when W. S. Gilbert tenderly addressed this dicky bird, his little tit mournfully replied, "Willow, titwillow, titwillow."

"I believe in two-faced truth," said Cyril Connolly (*The Unquiet Grave*), "in the Either, the Or, and the Holy Both."

DECEMBER.   The snow fell and fell, with ice fes-tooning the perishing trees, a glazed world. It took the flower-ing jasmine by surprise and a few violets. It took me by surprise because I consider North Carolina too tropical for snow and ice. Besides, these are the halcyon days, when the lady halcyon lays her eggs in a nest floating on the sea, and the wind is becalmed that she may hatch them. We are owed fourteen days of gentle weather, and this is what we get.

Eleanor drove me to town on a skating rink at ten miles an hour, since I couldn't get my car down the driveway, and a policeman brought me home, mannerly and brave. If we had to skid off the road and dive down an embankment, I figured, there couldn't be a nicer way to go than in the arms of the law. This morning a bee was in the hellebore.

Maybe movies and television do perform a handy service for the viewer, teaching him accommodation. One has the pleasure of watching dead people alive and healthy before one's eyes and listening to their voices—Gary Cooper forever in "High Noon," Marilyn Monroe in "Let's Make Love" and making it.

I asked a lady, "Do you mind seeing the dead there on the screen, walking about, living and breathing?" "Not in the least," she said astonished. "They're good actors."

1967

JANUARY. I gave my last examination of the term tonight, finishing at the stroke of ten, listened to two tragic confessions ("My mind went blank") and three speeches of love and gratitude ("You have changed my life"), came home and received a telephone call at midnight from a boy who cried "Have mercy." These are run-of-the-mill events. It doesn't occur to a student that his dilemma or delight has happened before, or that, if I have changed his life, it may be for better or for worse.

Rosa says Professor Boyce has been chasing squirrels. They annoy him by swishing around the flat roof of his modern house. The other day he caught one in a box trap and offered it to Rosa for squirrel stew. Before she could accept this delicious gift, it escaped by lifting the latch of the box.

"That squirrel was witty," said Rosa. "That squirrel outwitted the professor."

Tonight at the Easleys we had doves to eat, mourning-dove pie. None of us could face the dish (a gift from a doctor who spends his leisure out here in the country shooting the wood doves); but fortified by cocktails and the thought of ham sandwiches in the refrigerator to fall back on, we finally tackled it. It tasted like gamey chicken. I felt as if I were eating the Holy Ghost.

FEBRUARY. Writing is the same as looking in a mirror. I catch a sudden glimpse that considerably lowers my opinion of myself. Vanity tends to blind. The person reflected is diminished in appearance and small in talent, a dawdler. Why doesn't she comb her hair? Yet without a mirror, somebody said, one has no face. (And the face is gone as one backs away, and the mirror forgets.)

E. M. Forster, in his diary: "Am I modest or no?" Did he look to see?

David has made from a kit a plastic model of a man, a transparent male, complete with skeleton, lungs, liver, removable heart and intestines. But no genitals. He is an unmanned man, shy of the organs of increase. The two little boys noted the lack immediately but were polite about it, grateful for as much as they got.

David then followed this model of the visible man with one from another kit of an enormous visible eye. Pip stared hard at me and said, "Helen has an eye but it isn't like the model because her eye hasn't any numbers on it." After that we had a visible pigeon and a visible brain. The little boys asked me to choose what I would like to see next, and I said, "A visible woman."

"No," said David wearily. "Without her sex organs she isn't worth the trouble."

"White owls seem not to hoot at all," wrote Mr. White of Selborne, "but of this I am not positive." I envy him his concern, his absorption. He could go to bed at night thinking exclusively of owls, listening in the dark, not hearing any.

Without doubt, the men I most admire—Thoreau, Mr. White of Selborne, Montaigne—were solitary and unafraid. They kept their minds on white owls.

I have bought a pack of the wicked Tarot cards, fortune-telling cards, to take to class for demonstration when we read Eliot or Yeats. The students were amazed, disappointed, that I don't use them (like Madame Sosostris) for telling fortunes, not theirs or my own either.

"The only magic in them is literary," I say. "The last thing I want to know is my fate and my fortune."

"But Yeats *used* them."

"And what did he find out?"

I'm not above trying a little magic. I have a glass vial from the Castalian spring at Delphi, brimful of the water of inspiration. I have a magic stone, gray with white crossings, from Merlin's cave in Tintagel. And a string of worry beads from Athens.

MARCH. F. L. Lucas wrote (in *Style*) that among intellectuals the notion is that "taste consists of distaste." It's fashionable, I see, to disdain places, those the tourists have taken up. Edmund Wilson speaks with scorn of Delphi as a shabby little town and ignores Parnassus above his head. Christopher Isherwood condescends to the Pyramids, which look to him "ugly and quite new, like the tip-heaps of a prosperous quarry." The face of the Sphinx disgusts him, a "scarred and blinded baboon."

Both sound arrogant, more provincial than the tourists and much more disrespectful. Neither is a man to be trusted to enjoy himself.

William Plomer is impolite to the sea. It is all slop and thud to him. In his autobiography *At Home*, he writes, "Not that one can love the sea . . . it is oppressively elemental, and a great fidget." Wallace Stevens, who has made exquisite poetry of "The ever-hooded, tragic-gestured sea," betrays certain reservations in prose, "The thing itself is dirty, wobbly and wet." Oscar Wilde crossed the Atlantic Ocean in 1882 and said, "I am not exactly pleased with the Atlantic, it is not so majestic as I expected." Henry James "loathed and despised the sea." Baudelaire: "*Je te hais, Océan!*"

Tennyson took the trouble to visit the Swiss Alps, which pained him. They were tame and monotonous. Wordsworth on his European tour in 1790 went to Schaffhausen to view the magnificent roaring falls of the Rhine. "I had raised my ideas too high," said this lover of cataracts. "I must confess I was disappointed."

D. H. Lawrence was rude to mountains, especially the big ones in Switzerland. In a letter to Lady Cynthia Asquith (23

October 1913) he wrote: "No, I can't do with mountains at close quarters—they are always in the way, and they are so stupid, never moving and never doing anything but obtrude themselves." Dr. Johnson had the same blind spot, calling a mountain "a considerable protuberance." Even, I suppose, the Delectable Mountains of the Lord.

V. S. Pritchett takes the prize. He is annoyed by people, human beings in general, and when he is on the go would have the globe all to himself. "One thing does annoy me: other tourists."

Travelers must be discontent.

My yard is a green vista of wild onions. A solitary grosbeak has been hanging about under the willow tree for two weeks, without companions or mate. I've spoken to him about his solitude, not recommending it: "Go find yourself a grosbeak."

APRIL.   My editor Henry Simon says that a phrase I used, "Along came the witch," would make a good title for a book. What kind of book—to frighten children? About Mrs. Ips of Ipswich, or Mrs. Green of Greenwich, or the terrible witch of Wichita?

With a mind bewitched by witches, I woke up in the middle of the night saying aloud (this is the God's truth), "Which wich is the Wich witch?"

> A witch may come from Connecticut
> Or Massachusetts properly, but
> From Kansas? No. It's against the law
> To be a witch from Wichita.

In Thessaly, where they once flourished, witches were supposed to be able to make the moon descend from the sky. Anybody can do that. Just look into a puddle.

———

All the wild witches, those most noble ladies,
For all their broomsticks and their tears,
Their angry tears, are gone.

—Yeats, "Lines Written in Dejection"

Yeats must have been dejected to write that lyrical nonsense. A known and certain fact about witches is their inability to shed tears. Angels weep, but witches and crocodiles never do.

Besides, what made him think the witches are gone? The only one missing (whose loss I deeply lament) is Shelley's noble Witch of Atlas, "A lovely lady garmented in light," who lived on Atlas mountain and sat on an emerald stone. She could change from a vapor to a cloud to a meteor to a star. She could tame wild beasts, teach baby lions to behave, make leopards gentle as a doe. But her real talent was to see into the souls of men within their mortal bodies. To those beautiful in spirit she gave a magic elixir in a crystal bowl. On the others, incurably ugly of soul, she used her witchery to make a fool of a priest, inspire a king to put his crown on an ape, tempt soldiers to beat their swords to ploughshares, while she kept

The tenor of her contemplation calm,
With open eyes, closed feet, and folded palm.

Here I've looked forward to Wallace Stevens's *Letters* and Harold Nicolson's *Diaries and Letters*. I love letters and diaries, not expecting them to be dull, or that a writer will keep a dreary journal or send off stupidities to his wife by post. The marvel is that people write well *any* of the time. It seems not to be instinctive or natural.

Nicolson sounds bluff but fastidious, a snob. He didn't like to touch people. Stevens sounds cold, unable to express love or perhaps not feeling it. Instead of being more real, understandable, human, both men are reduced in size. There is Nicolson writing his wife, December 2, 1936, "How I hate and detest women," adding he didn't mind women like her (what was she? Mannish in dress, lesbian in habit). "I *loathe* women," he went on. "The only thing that will make them behave decently is to give them complete equality and no privileges. Now they claim equality *plus* privileges. They let us down: they let us down all the time. They are beasts. I loathe them." Bluff is the word.

Wallace Stevens says a few good things, like "God is gracious to some very peculiar people."

After reading my piece "Hellgazers and Rejoicers" in the New York *Times Book Review*, where I said I was by nature a rejoicer, having announced in an earlier piece I was by nature a hellgazer ("To live in hell and heaven to behold"), Father Bertrand Weaver sent me his paperback *JOY*. "Please shout for joy!" he advised, underlining it three times. The table of contents lists 22 kinds of joy, all unfortunately pious. I am thankful, though, to find there are so many, even "The Joy of Pain."

MAY.   General Westmoreland made a speech in New York on the escalation of the war in Vietnam: "I was delighted to hear that the Mig airbase has been bombed." *Delighted.* Loud and happy applause came from the diners, one of them a chaplain seated next the General. "It is one of the most gratifying episodes of the war," said a Senator.

Westmoreland as military commander called it a war of attrition, to kill more of them than kill us. (A war of escalation too with Indochina?)

Prince of Verona (*Romeo and Juliet*): "Seal up the mouth of outrage for a while."

I drove to Charlottesville this morning to my family's bosom. The Virginia thrush was singing and three small children sat in a row on the doorstep waiting for me. I left my empty days behind—like crossing a bridge.

David and Peggy took me to three student parties, the kind of thing I carefully avoid at home. I learned my mistake in staying away, for these brief researches were encouraging. Nothing has changed since I was in college. On Friday night at a hangout called the Prism we saw a one-act play written by a student, where a boy and girl sat on a sofa and discussed sleeping together. (They called it that, sleeping.) I blinked my ears. Every word they said might have been written in the 1920's (and was)—the same pleading argument by the boy, the same high-principled objections by the girl who was temporarily defending her virtue, eager to lose it yet keep the whole thing on a lofty plane. She would lose it in the end, one was led to hope, if they ever stopped talking.

A poet with straggly beard and sheepdog hair said he would introduce a novel experiment by reading his poems to guitar accompaniment. Man, where have you been?

On Saturday, two male Virginia students in bright plaid trousers gave a noisy cocktail party in their apartment. On arrival we were led straight to the bathroom, done in psychedelic colors and large photographs of funky nudes, all female. At Greenwich Village parties when I was a graduate student, we *always* had to admire the bathroom, a symbol of uninhibited creative art. One, I remember, was done in black, another in sybaritic lavender. With nudes.

The third party on Sunday in the gymnasium was a protest party of the serious longhairs. I never heard what they were protesting besides Vietnam, as we all are. Here everyone looked glum, drank warm beer out of paper cups, the men hairy, the girls stringy and wan. Nobody grew cheerful or abusive, even argumentative. In this Jeffersonian landscape, something was missing; perhaps Jefferson was. (Yet he is the one who said, "A little rebellion now and then is a good thing.")

So, like Wallace Stevens "Waving Adieu, Adieu, Adieu," I went back home to find I am two distinct people: sociable and solitary.

IT IS POSSIBLE, POSSIBLE, POSSIBLE

What I tell you three times is true
Said Wallace Stevens, "Waving adieu, adieu, adieu."
Three times, said E. E. Cummings, this is so:

"And all the world is joyless joyless joyless." Oh,
Three times cried Mallarmé, "*L'azur! L'azur! L'azur!
L'azur!*" I can't count.

J U N E .   Lucrece who was raped said, "I am the mistress
of my fate." So that is where W. E. Henley got it, changing the
sex to praise himself, "I am the master of my fate, I am the
captain of my soul." Neither of them told the truth anyway.
Today one says, "I am the victim of my fate, I am the loser
of my soul."

I shall send the quotation to Henry Simon about being
mistress of my fate, since we've been arguing for years over
words like *bardess* and *authoress* and other indignities to
describe women. I've sent him some beauties, such as *globe
trotteress, villainess, clerkess, inventress, philosophess, loveress,*
and *fornicatress,* all found in books written by men. He ap-
proves of these condescensions as fair and appropriate.

The only word I will allow is *mistress,* which is something
a man can't very well be. And I will allow *witch.*

> Such great achievements cannot fail
> To cast salt on a woman's tail.   —*Hudibras*

I listened for an hour tonight to four poets on educational
television, Stanley Kunitz, Marianne Moore, Howard Nemerov,
and Robert Graves. They couldn't have lasted ten minutes on
commercial television—no plot, no passion, no violence.

Marianne Moore in a tricorne hat trembled with old age at
eighty, speaking in a feeble, staggering voice. I caught only
a word or two.

Robert Graves spoke with scorn of Keats and Blake, which
ill became him. He looked like an old lady himself with a mop
of white hair. He frowned in distaste. His tone was lordly,
bemused by the Muse.

On the subject of the evening, "Poetry—for whom?," Howard
Nemerov said, "Baby, if you have to ask the question, you

don't want the answer." Mr. Kunitz referred to him as a wit.
Nemerov then read some sententious remarks prepared ahead
of time and written out. This bored his associates, who looked
bored.

They were a pitiful crew. The modern poet is unpopular,
Kunitz said in stammers; he doesn't appeal. "Why should anybody want to listen to the poets? Does the poet serve any
function at all?"

"Poetry is the primary purpose of language," said Nemerov,
having written it down ahead of time. "O.K.?" he added.

Miss Moore observed that people don't look for substance
in poetry.

Graves said poetry should make the hair stand on end. Full
of furor poeticus, his hair was already doing that.

Nemerov interrupted him to read "Lion and Honeycomb,"
which he called a "nasty, meanminded poem" about being a
poet and thinking: God! all this *garbage*. He said it was about
disgust with poetry. "What did I get into it for?"

"Love and poetry are synonymous," said Graves in cold
reproof. As if to freshen the air he launched into a love poem
of his making. He had the most applause.

"We're nothing at all without convictions," whispered
Marianne Moore at the end. But what did any of them offer
as convictions? They performed a farce. I enjoyed it very much.

"I am still amused at the paradox of poetry's obstinate
continuance in the present phase of civilization."
—Robert Graves, *The White Goddess*

JULY.   David is teaching Tudor Drama and Shakespeare
at Harvard. We have rented for the summer a house on Common Street, Belmont. I like living on a common street, near a
Catholic church that plays "The Rosary" at sundown on an
electric carillon. The house is uncommon with five bathrooms,
a fact which describes not opulence but size. As we accustom

ourselves to multiple possessions and gadgets—electric dishwasher, electric can opener, garbage disposal (or refusal), few of which work—I say to Peggy, "What would a stranger think who came to live in my house?"

"That you had moved everything to the attic."

Evenings, David's graduate students come to talk, argue, pontificate, needing to be sent home like undergraduates, who never learn to tell time. You would think they could dispose of literature by midnight. They are young and intense, the girls no longer the wispy spinsters of my day, but how deadly in earnest. They prefer the scholarly pursuit to flirtation, again proving they aren't yet grown up. ("Women run to extremes," said La Bruyère, a bachelor.)

Or we attend parties given by friends on the faculty—Howard Mumford Jones, Herschel Baker. The difference between socializing with faculty and with students is that with students I take care to establish my identity as teacher. Otherwise they will mistake me for the grandmother down from the garret and flee in haste. The young condescend to somebody's "parent," to be avoided as a trap, a conversational hazard.

Herschel Baker tells me he doesn't want women in Harvard's graduate school, and I bristle. We weren't wanted in my time either. Now it's worse, says Baker. Formerly after finishing her degree, a woman would go off and get married, have children and grow flowers if she had a chance. Now she will marry and *still* want to teach, preferably in the vicinity of her husband. Women are such problems.

Stephen at five says: "I want to be a bird because I want to be never caught." He makes me tremble, a child who knows he can't catch a bird but will be caught himself.

Pip at four, home from nursery school with a cold, brought me a pile of snippets of paper.

"What are they?"

"Gables," he said.

"Don't they need a house?"

He went off for a while and returned with a series of whirls that didn't please him. "A Japanese house," he said. "They don't have gables."

So I drew a large square house with a high roof. Across the top he carefully pasted seven gables.

Kate the Shrew saw herself in a movie, "The Taming of the Shrew." All three children witnessed with approval the story of Kate's misbehavior and subduing, Kate the Bold and Kate the Tamed. Our Kate sat on the edge of her seat to watch Elizabeth Taylor and saw herself. "That's Kate," she murmured with complacence at the pummeling by Petruchio. She is two and a half.

"Kiss me, Kate," we say, loving her.

Robert Lowell read his poetry tonight in Sanders Theater, America's "greatest living poet," who ought to work on his performance and his manners. He has been giving poetry readings for a quarter of a century but hasn't yet learned how to read aloud. He writes that the four needs for oral performance are these: humor, shock, narrative, and a hypnotic voice. Then, strangely enough, he misses them all, mumbling with face down, dodging the microphone, letting a line fade away unheard. Outside Memorial Hall a thunderstorm raged, sirens screamed, tires squealed. Robert Lowell fumed at the competition. His mood worsened to growling despair. Why not accept tumult and shout it down as proper accompaniment to chaos?

With a volume of his poems in my lap, I could follow the fine but inaudible poem about his illness as an inmate at McLean's hospital outside Boston,

> My heart grows tense
> as though a harpoon were sparring for the kill.
> (This is the house for the "mentally ill.")

"What use is my sense of humor?" the poem goes on to ask. And there in my mind was James Thurber's comment about F. Scott Fitzgerald after his crack-up, "A sense of humor might have saved him."

His poems are wounds inflicted by a wounded man. With-

out compassion for himself, he can write with powerful pity
for us all:

> Pity the planet, all joy gone
> from this sweet, volcanic cone.

A U G U S T .   I came home alone by Whisperjet, 600 miles
an hour, writing verse to keep from weeping. B. died three
years ago today, August 16.

> The man on the Whisperjet,
> Winging homeward by jet propulsion, saw her
> Face in his glass, hummed "The Flight of the Bumblebee,"
> Whispered a line of Keats smilingly
> "Away! away! for I will fly to thee,"
> And flew to her, arriving by Whisperjet
> Nonstop from LaGuardia.

After Henry Simon's third heart attack, he has retired as
editor from Simon and Schuster and turned me over to Hiram
Haydn of Harcourt, Brace. I used to write verse at Hiram's
request for *The American Scholar,* and like everyone else I
love him. Hiram no sooner agreed to read my manuscript than
he had a heart attack during a holiday in New Mexico. I am
the Black Widow. Destruction follows in my path. Sorrow is
so faithful to me and so kind.

No birds sing. August is the mute month. Comatose.

S E P T E M B E R .   The first English Department party
of the season was at the Duffeys, the identical professors, their
identical wives. And Helen alone, damn it. I go from solitude
to multitude, feeling afterward like a flagellant, recalling my
struts and inanities, full of consequence and plume (Charles
Lamb: "How I like to be liked, and what I *do* to be liked!")
Then mellowness sets in, and along comes the next party.

Anyone not invited is either a cur or an outcast. Were there a Footman, he would snicker at the door.

THE SUSPECT

I saw her there myself
All cockled up for Sunday,
Astrut to the naked eye,
Riotous and randy,
But hesitated to
Call and inform the police,
Though this poor woman, I knew,
Was—being I—the one who.

Time comes round for a schoolday, the scurry of scholars, the chasing of mayflies. But not the same learners, no, this is no mockery. Each year they are younger, on hand to better their minds or whatever we expect them to do, and I tell the new arrivals they have only two things to learn in this course: how to read and how to write. The shock is visible when they discover I mean how to read Chaucer, about whom up to now they've been content to know nothing. When did he live? "Seventh century," they guess, "seventeenth?" What language did he write? "Anglo-Saxon," they presume, "or German." "Mrs. Bevington, this isn't English!"

The outcome is certain—they will be won, his captive for life. They always are. Through a trip to Canterbury with the Miller, the Wife of Bath, the Parson, they absorb both bawdy and *gentilesse*.

Not so long ago students came to college saying "I love poetry." They waited after class to present their credentials and breathe the words in my ear to prove it: "How do I love thee? Let me count the ways."

"What is the second line?" I would ask.

Nobody could remember.

Bunthorne: "Tell me, girl, do you ever yearn?"

Patience (misunderstanding him): "I earn my living."

O C T O B E R .   Hiram Haydn telephoned me from New York. I love your book, he said, I love it *[A Book and a Love Affair]*. "The very things you write about happened to me as a student at Columbia. I too fell in love. I too took a walk in the Catskills with Professor Ernest Hunter Wright. I too read with rapture Thoreau and Montaigne. So if we can agree upon terms we are ready to offer you a contract." The voice of salvation. No words are more paradisal except in a real love affair.

Hiram Haydn has a secretary Miss Brahms.

"It won't happen in my lifetime," B. used to say. And he was right. The worst disasters, after all, didn't happen: the planet delayed coming to an end, World War III failed to begin, nobody got lost on his way to the moon, no one whom B. loved deeply died. He was spared a few ultimate tragedies.

But what of the lifetime of his sons? Is there comfort or hope in what he so confidently said? Sure there is. The way to live is the way B. lived. He suffered no failure of nerve and no worry about destiny.

Take the tick and the flea. Colin Falck, a contemporary English poet (or proser) wrote "The Tick," which appeared in last week's *Times Literary Supplement*. Since he intended it for a poem and a poem consists of an arrangement of lines however arbitrary, Mr. Falck arranged it (and the *TLS* for inscrutable reasons of its own printed it) like this:

THE TICK

When a suitable host passes within reach
It attaches itself
And feeds for from two to eight days.
Removal, at this stage, is not possible
By force. The attempt may leave
The delicate feeding-mechanism embedded in the wound.
When the process is complete, and the parasite's body
Distended with blood, it falls to the ground
Of its own accord. The host

Is not materially harmed, though in rare cases
The bite may cause paralysis and death.
It can survive for long periods without food.

Well, not all poems have to be about love, but it helps.

John Donne wrote "The Flea"—a *song*, a love song, about a flea. (In his day poetry was distinguishable from prose.) When Donne urges his girl in vain to make love with him and they are bit by the same flea, he tells her, "Don't you see how easy it is? This flea has united us, no harm done, though you said No. It is our temple and our marriage bed."

> Marke but this flea, and marke in this,
> How little that which thou deny'st me is;
> It suck'd me first, and now sucks thee,
> And in this flea, our two bloods mingled bee;
> Thou know'st that this cannot be said
> A sinne, nor shame, nor losse of maidenhead,
> 　　Yet this enjoyes before it wooe,
> 　　And pamper'd swells with one blood made of two,
> 　　And this, alas, is more than wee would doe.

Yeats wrote a couplet once to describe his opinion of Augustine Birrell:

> He's grown to be a master of the trick
> That turns a lively flea into a tick.

It seems to make more sense to me now.

NOVEMBER.　A story of the generation gap: Newton Minow, Mr. Kennedy's head of Federal Communications Commission, stopped a girl after class at Columbia University where he teaches a course to say, "I am just old enough to be embarrassed by that pin you're wearing, 'MAKE LOVE, NOT WAR.'"

"But you don't understand!" she cried. "We don't mean a lay. We mean the Brotherhood of Man."

That night at dinner Minow told the story to Walter Lippmann. Lippmann gave it sober thought. "What is a lay?" he
asked.

Minow went home and related the whole episode to his
teenage daughter. She stared at him puzzled. "Who is Walter
Lippmann?" she said.

You have to be in the middle to see both ends.

The *Times Literary Supplement* is useful for its habit of
printing fair examples of the most authentic and most original
non-poetry now being written, or perhaps ever written in the
history of poetry. This one is called "Sure" by Hugo Williams:

> Walking upstairs after breakfast
> I looked round to see if you were following
> And caught sight of you
> Turning the corner with a tray
> As I closed the bathroom door.

That strong last line! "Sure" must mean he knew where
he had to go.

In class I read aloud the opening lines of John Donne's
holy sonnet:

> What if this present were the world's last night?
> Marke in my heart, O Soule, where thou dost dwell.

"Where did Donne's soul dwell?" I asked a daydreamer.
Gaping astonished at his book, he said he didn't know. "Then,
where does *your* soul dwell?" You would think I had asked
the location of his phallus (not that he would recognize the
word) as, abashed, he shook his head. No soul. The rest of
the class, eager to locate its immortal soul, placed it variously
in the head, heart, or ribcage till at death it flies out the
mouth and away. One student thought his resided in his
liver. "Or the pineal gland," I said. So we went on reading
Donne.

The soul is adroit, a slippery essence or entity to track down.
St. Isidore, who kept bees, believed even the stars have a soul.
In the seventeenth century, scientists tried to discover the heft

of the soul by weighing a man just before and just after death. No significant figures were obtained.

This talk of souls led me to read a book by Eugène Marais, *The Soul of the White Ant*. (He also wrote *The Soul of the Ape* after spending three years in Africa making friends with wild baboons.) What is known as psyche or soul, says Marais, is beyond reach of our senses. "No one has ever seen or smelt, or heard or tasted or felt the psyche, or even a piece of it." Marais calls *soul* and *life* two words for the same thing. When one of them dies so does the other, which is hardly a theological view.

The white ant has a group soul; no termite can act alone. Men and baboons, on the contrary, have either lost, inhibited, or paralyzed the herd instinct. Man, with the soul of a primate, acts singly, adapts himself to new environments. But the price of independence comes high, Marais believes, and will lead to the extinction of man and ape, his soul included.

I shan't tell my students, certainly not. This is a poetry course.

DECEMBER. Now that David is a professor of English at the University of Chicago, I return to a university from which I graduated years ago and haven't seen since. It's an uneasy journey, a triple threat to visit three of my lives, all spent within a few city blocks of each other.

The first time, I was a child staying one long unhappy summer with Charley, who moved to Chicago's South Side in 1915. When I didn't write her, Lizzie got it into her outraged head that Charley had kidnaped me and threatened to bring in the Bureau of Investigation (later called the FBI) and have him arrested. The ruckus made Charley laugh, since kidnaping me was the last thing that would occur to him. The second time, I was an undergraduate at Chicago, estranged from my father, living without his knowledge in the same city. The third time—who am I?—mother of David who teaches the Shakespeare course I once took (and fell in love with the professor) and for love ought to take again, round and round the dizzy wheel.

The little artist's studio on East 57th Street where I lived as a student at the University is gone, gone, gone. It was left over from the World's Fair of 1893, a one-room shop with plate-glass window across the front. Now nothing remains of that rustic row of shacks (Floyd Dell had lived in mine and written *Moon Calf*), only an empty lot, tall grass and weeds, only a streetsign. As in a nightmare, I search and can't find the place. I hope after a while one stops being haunted.

At a Hyde Park party last night, I met my old professor, Napier Wilt, who had the puzzled air of a man vainly searching his memory. During the evening he would saunter up, look me over, and remark, "She's a former student of mine."

As he left, he said, "Helen Smith? Ah, yes, yes, of course I remember you perfectly, Helen Smith." The whiskey did it: he recalled nothing. Nor did I recognize him. When I knew him, I had the starry eyes of a nineteen-year-old; the time he came to tea he seemed so lean, sardonic, dashing, I was speechless. What do you say to a man who teaches you Whitman and Poe? You pass the cinnamon toast and brood about his love life. Now he is plump, bald, retired, a confirmed bachelor of seventy-two.

A doormat on sale in a gift shop says, "Go Away." Stephen, a generous child, says, "Maybe the word Welcome is on the other side."

Kenneth Koch and his wife came to dinner. He is of the New York School of contemporary poets, though he seemed at home tonight in Chicago. Someone said, "You'll adore him. He's a riot!" He was a riot, and we did. He had a mop of curly hair, an unceasing flow of talk, shop talk, obsessive talk, *me* talk. He must be delightful chaos to live with, a daily tumult. His wife was wordless till, in a flurry of his words, they went away.

Koch is a funny man, if only he wouldn't go on so long.

In *Thank You and Other Poems,* he begins, "Is the basketball coach a homosexual lemon manufacturer?" In "Taking a Walk with You" he tells of his capacity for misunderstanding. "I thought Axel's Castle was a garage. . . . I misunderstood childhood. . . . I misunderstand generally Oklahoma and Arkansas. . . . I misunderstand you." After four pages of this, he says, "I love you, but it is difficult to stop writing."

And there was a formal black-tie Guggenheim party at the Congress tonight (David is a Guggenheim scholar), where I met Robert Lowell. As the honored guest, who was to be the speaker of the evening, he was dressed in an old tan corduroy jacket, unpressed pants, checked blue shirt, red bow tie. His thinning gray hair was tousled, his spectacles slipped down his nose, as if he had just jumped up from his writing desk. But would a surgeon attend in rubber gloves, a painter in his smock?

Over a cocktail he took my free hand and fondled it, addressing me as Cousin, under the impression, I think, that I was Fanny Patton, who is his cousin. Or this may be his Elizabethan way with women. He said he was coming to Duke University in the spring to give a poetry reading. Then he asked the question that proves he really is a poet.

"When *is* spring?" asked Robert Lowell.

I laughed and didn't tell him.

Peggy has been calling her kindly postman Mr. Littlejohn each day, to his face. Lately she discovered his name is actually Mr. Hightower. He has delivered the mail on time and taken no offense.

A satisfactory Christmas, as the Magus said.

But a thin pale Chinese student at the A. & P. was buying a single holiday item, one frozen Chinese TV dinner.

1968

JANUARY.   I know a generous man, a benevolist. On
June 17, 1962, Glenway Wescott wrote me a three-page letter
on "shocking pink" paper to say he liked *When Found, Make
a Verse Of* and asked me to go on finding and making more
of the same. Today, 5½ years later, he sent a four-page letter
on identical pink paper, written at 4:00 A.M., to say he had
reread the book without surfeit and liked it better than before.
No one has ever written me twice about the same book or,
for that matter, written me anything at four in the morning.

The new Poet Laureate is Cecil Day Lewis, Poet to the
Monarch. I respect the choice for one reason: you wouldn't
find America honoring a former Communist, member of the
Party. The other possibility, it seems, was John Betjeman;
but levity in a court poet is worse than disloyalty to the
Crown. He might have written verses in praise of the Queen's
sturdy legs, or panted for her on a tennis court.
    However, I wish they would change the office to Keeper
of the Queen's Swans.

A child now aged five will be graduated in the Class of
1984. That is our Pip. He will be able to test George Orwell's
predictions for the hellbent state of the world of 1984, proving
Orwell inventive but wrong, in fact, and the world worse off
than he or anyone could have conceived. *1984* was published
back in 1949 to warn of the horrors of a future police state.
The Berlin Wall was beyond his invention, as were so *many*
big brothers with their eyes fastened upon us.

FEBRUARY.   The film "Zorba the Greek" is the movie
they love and go to see twice. Tonight the line of students
outside the Quadrangle Theater extended past the library.

189

What is it that appeals to them? Two students have told me I remind them of Zorba, which is my reason for going to find out why. I appreciate the compliment of resembling a grizzled, dirty, ignorant, loud-mouthed Cretan (Anthony Quinn), who made love freely, danced solo, fought, showed off, and in general found life good no matter what the terms.

Nikos Kazantzakis, who wrote *Zorba the Greek*, was born in Crete, in Heraklion (so was El Greco. Why did they call him The Greek, not The Cretan?). When he died in 1957 he was buried above the city on the old Venetian wall, with this epitaph of his making:

> I hope for nothing.
> I fear nothing.
> I am free.

Robert Payne, in *The Isles of Greece*, says the words appear on a thousand ancient Greek tombs: "I was not. I came to be. I am not. I care not." Kazantzakis wanted to die a Greek.

"Those who do not understand the past are doomed to relive it," said Goethe. I might apply the fault to myself and my books—except here is another highsounding reflection with no more truth than untruth, neither so nor not so. (Say it any way you like, in reverse or upside down.) Those who fail to understand the past may simply refuse or neglect to relive it, as is their right. Others relive it with no sense of doom. And so on. Goethe's words are full of surface wisdom.

There's a hippie in my modern poetry class, front row. He is longhaired, bearded, barefoot, wayout, scruffy, and ramshackle, crouched and waiting a chance to protest. He knows I'm a square. But since I've been defending the rebels and protesters (Auden), the grubby young bohemians (Dylan Thomas), and the Surrealists to boot, so far he has been frustrated—till today.

"Why did you say the Dadaists were a sick group?" he called out.

"It's a compliment, isn't it?"

Next he will start to cut class, appearing spasmodically,

turning in any written papers four weeks late on a subject unrelated to literature. It is his only way to show rejection of the system. He will misspell, misquote, misunderstand what he reads, and expect an A in the course. He saves his love for love-ins. I rather like him.

"I used to be bright," says Elwood P. Dowd to his rabbit Harvey. "Now I am only pleasant."

Isak Dinesen makes an extravagant claim (they all do. It's an occupational hazard of writers): "With the exception of God, I believe in absolutely nothing whatever."

A piece of bombast. She believed in herself as a writer and, apparently, as an aphorist. If she believed in God, as stated, she necessarily believed in a great deal—in love, I should think. Isn't God love?

Fannie Hurst is dead at 78. I met her in New York at a party a hundred years ago and was struck then, at my first conscious meeting with the literary Ego, by how confidently she played the part of professional writer. She dressed for it, walked, talked like Fannie Hurst. She performed the star role with the assurance of one who knew she could write (she couldn't), who was different in kind, an artist set apart and dedicated. She called her autobiography *Anatomy of Me: A Wonderer in Search of Herself.*

Her marriage too was different. She and her husband lived in separate establishments for thirty-seven years. When he wanted to see her, he had to arrange a meeting by telephone. "A marriage happier than most," she said of it. I don't know what he said. No children.

Our wrathful and enraged Governor Moore of North Carolina, the tobacco state, attacks the U.S. Public Health anti-smoking campaign. He denounces it as "a massive effort by our government to cripple one of the nation's greatest industries." He exposes it as a skulking base attempt to destroy our lives and livelihood down here, not for a moment asking how many lives cigarettes will destroy. The poor benighted South, guilty and unashamed.

We make millions of cigarettes in Durham. Back in the 1880's, the Bull Durham tobacco factory was the largest in the world. People came from miles around to admire the snorting bull painted on the factory and listen to the steam whistle imitating his bellow. It cost $6 every time the whistle blew.

MARCH.   Hiram Haydn sent me the jacket for *A Book and a Love Affair*. He found it unusual. I found it unusual. The designer had taken the first page of my manuscript and made the jacket from it, with words I had crossed out or written in. I found it messy, agreeably so. It glistens with the sweat of composition. At the moment Harcourt, Brace calls the book a *novel*. Woe, I say, have I written a novel? I'm glad they think it a story (why else would one read it?), but fiction? No, it isn't fictive or fabulous, not a word invented. There were memories enough to meet the need.

The galley proofs show me adverb drunk, plastered with adverbs, reeling with them, obsessed by two adjectives: *terrible* and *splendid*. I walk the floor trying to think of synonyms. A terrible thing is terrible. There is no substitute for splendor.

F. L. Lucas says the word "lad" is repeated 67 times in *A Shropshire Lad*, thereby making is unusable for generations to come.

> Though all my wares bee trash,
> > The hart is true,
> > The hart is true,
> > The hart is true. (Anon.)

APRIL.   This is a dark day, April 4, when Martin Luther King was shot and killed by a white sniper. As King stood on a balcony of a motel in Memphis, he was murdered, like Gandhi destroyed by violence, a man pleading for nonviolence in the world and for his people. And from his death comes more death.

Rioting and killing have broken out. Here at home rampaging and burning strike our streets, black against white, racism. Tension fouls the air. And fear, with street riots by Negroes made manic for revenge, responding with hate. They have set a number of fires, wrecking stores along Ninth Street out my way. When I stopped at a filling station for gas after school, the attendant warned me to go somewhere and hide. "If a nigger comes near me," he said, "I'll kill him with my bare hands!"

All this because a man died who sought peace and love. "I have a dream," he said. Langston Hughes asked:

> What happens to a dream deferred?
> Does it dry up like a raisin in the sun? . . .
> *Or does it explode?*

We've had a curfew for the last four nights, 7:00 P.M. to 5:00 A.M. (greatly inconveniencing milkmen and paper carriers, the most nonviolent travelers in the dark). I feel imprisoned in silence at home, numbed at school.

Things fall apart. Some two hundred students marched to President Knight's house, bearing a petition he refused to sign. For one thing, they demanded he resign from the segregated Hope Valley Country Club, seeing no irony in belonging themselves to Greek letter fraternities and sororities. After camping in his living room for two days and nights, till Knight collapsed and went to hospital (where he was variously reported as having a breakdown, dying, resigning), they moved to headquarters on West Campus in front of the Chapel and our benefactor's statue. Wouldn't Buck Duke be astonished at their cheek?

Now the students are holding a Vigil, spending the nights on the quadrangle in bedrolls and sleeping bags, avoiding classes, dressed like flower children with love beads and armbands—some with balloons or an Easter bunny—listening to hate speeches while they sing "We Shall Overcome." The Vigil has lasted four days and nights, during which it poured rain. Joan Baez flew in to play her guitar and talk freedom over the loudspeaker. But the students are uneasy in a performance or demonstration for which as revolutionaries they are unrehearsed. They are supposed to be fighting the Establishment, in a crusade against "University injustice." What conformity is required of rebels!

A girl telephones, "Mrs. Bevington, I'm at the Vigil. Are you in your office?" "Yes, I'm holding my Vigil here." She dashes over between speeches, dressed in beads and bright colors, and dutifully fills out her schedule of courses for the fall term. She looks flushed, radiant, and a bit shamefaced. Placards in the hall remind the rioters of the annual "Joe College Weekend," which will be the next fling or revel— picnics, rock music, balloons . . .

A few of the faculty take part, joining the protest, trying to hold classes (about what?) on the edge of the mob. Faculty wives serve fried chicken and mashed potatoes. The numbers yesterday were said to reach 1,600. "We'll get national attention," someone says. "I wonder why we're doing it?" one student asks another.

Five-year-old Pip sent me an Easter card with a picture of Raphael's three graces, naked, fleshly, and beautiful. On the other side he had laboriously printed the words "For Martin Luther King" and signed it "Pip love." He said at the tragic news, "It is not a very good life to be a dead person."

Last night Philip my son arrived. He flew from Palo Alto on his way to Physics meetings in Washington and Philadelphia, a week away from home. I find it unbearable to travel alone, and I am on my feet. What would I dare to do in a wheel chair?

We talked all the waking hours. At 6:00 P.M. I stood beside him as he waited to be carried up the boarding steps to his plane. Now in the house are the marks of his chair. Wherever I look is proof that he came and that he went away. The gods have given him courage. The gods make me solitary and afraid.

That he surmounts, so this may I. So this must I.

M A Y.   The worst violence has moved to Columbia University, a six-day rebellion, a disaster area, with fighting, bloodshed, the taking over of buildings with the battle cry "Student Power," finally the closing down of a paralyzed university—the new familiar meaningless pattern. Had it happened when I was a student there, nothing, nobody, could have led me to riot or even to shake my fist. I was no joiner of movements or promoter of causes, nor was B. given to following the mob. One thing is clear: it is no place now for a book and a love affair.

Duke is proud of our reputation for polite, orderly protest. We look rational if set beside Berkeley, Wisconsin, Columbia, hundreds of colleges torn apart with outbreaks like explosions in a warstricken country. Our sanity is relative, a poor boast that we haven't yet killed or destroyed anybody. A campus is the arena where we are busy righting the wrongs of the world.

Edith Sitwell said, "You need never grow old except in your body." She couldn't be the best authority, not having been young, having died a virgin. Yeats is the one to listen to. He said it many times, "Grant me an old man's frenzy." And I say it. A little frenzy music, please, not the violence of the young.

My examination in modern poetry came this morning, three hours of inner tussle, which led the sufferers to remove their shoes and wiggle their toes. It is odd: some are struck with absolute wonder (at Yeats, say); others never hear a thing.

Afterward a student came to the desk. "Is it true you've written a book?"

"Yes."

"About yourself?"

"Yes."

"That's what my roommate told me. He said you had written a whole entire book about yourself. Is it like Yeats?"

"Oh no, of course not. He was a poet."

"My roommate said it was sort of weird like Yeats. Like 'The Wild Old Wicked Man.'"

"Give your roommate my love."

The *Times Literary Supplement* now speaks of a stool volume. In a review of *The Letters of Groucho Marx* (why on earth descend to them?), the critic calls it "a splendid stool or bedside volume." Read one letter at a time, he advises, "with an interval for relish."

J U N E .   Harmon telephoned me from New York. "Is this your voice?" he said, and I laughed with joy to hear from an old friend. Then something like a catch in his voice made me ask, "What is wrong?"

"Haven't you heard? It's Robert Kennedy. He was shot."

So we die a little more each time. We hear news of murder, bloody assassination, senseless killing, while shopping at the A. & P., by telephone, over television. We reach out to one another, touching each other's hand. We say, "My God, what next?"

Robert Kennedy was killed by a young Jordanian Arab in the Ambassador Hotel in Los Angeles. A night or two ago Walter Cronkite, commenting on the news of the world (the failure of the peace talks, the riots in Paris) said, "It may yet overwhelm us all."

Dr. Johnson in 1783: "Why I am now come to that time when I wish all bitterness and animosity to be at an end." In a few months he was dead, having reached too soon (or too late?) the fulfillment of his desire.

J U L Y .   In spite of a planet beset like ours, I still harp on
happiness, peace, love. Colette's husband, Maurice Goudeket,
has written a book on happiness, *The Delights of Growing
Old*, a brash, disheartening title. I hope it sounds appealing in
French. (It does: *La Douceur de Vieillir*.)

Happiness is breathing, not to be confused with the kind of
wellbeing derived from physical comforts like refrigerators
full of beer, or from electric mixers. This kind you breathe in
and out. A layer of air holds you up and you soar above
paltriness to become beneficent. It is respiratory.

"Begin by getting used to breathing deeply. . . . At each
inward breath, say to yourself, 'I am breathing, so I am
happy.'" (To say "So I am not dead" would be to take a
negative view.)

Charming man. I must try it sometime. But what euphoric
air is one to breathe instead of smog and air pollution?

A sign on the North Carolina highway says, "Be kind to
yourself."

I wanted to give my Oldsmobile to David. That meant
buying a new car, a smaller one. As usual I balked at gadgets.
No airconditioning, please. No radio. No clock. Just a blue
car, no trimmings. The salesman whistled in unbelief. "You
can't *buy* a car without airconditioning, madam, not an Oldsmobile. We haven't got one in stock. It would take a special
order, delay of months." So I meekly submitted, hoping to
forget the knobs and controls. Now the temperature is 96°,
I ride along cool as a blue goose, shut in, victimized. (It
has no clock.)

Notice the entries—I, I, I, alone, alone, alone.

Nobody is around but me and a mockingbird. He is busy
with war, I with peace. Seeing his image reflected in the study
window, he beats his wings like a whirlwind to frighten the
enemy and rout him. After a while the flutter and peck destroy
my peace and I become the enemy. I rush out the door
waving my arms. Aha! Just as he thought with that bird-
brain—this bird is after him. Before I am back in the house

he swoops down from the dogwood tree ready for a fight to the death.

At midnight the mockingbird is singing. At two in the morning he (and friends) is still at it, with pleasant twitters and chirps, an occasional high note of joy. At 4:00 A.M., not a sound; the concert is over and I sleep. At 4:10 A.M. the cardinal starts, "Cheer, cheer, cheer," the unbearably smug trill of an early riser.

AUGUST. If there is peace it is here at the Ohio farm on Stumpville Road near Jefferson, Ohio, where Peggy and David spend their summers. The three children are like birds in flight, filling the air with chittering, up and away, returning. They beam and squall. They have ordered from Sears, Roebuck a "Have-a-hart Animal Trap," a very dirty pun. So far they've captured two skunks and a cat. The directions say, if it's properly baited you can catch an armadillo.

Pip sits at a table beside me to write his book. He looks at my typewriter and says, "Helen, how many pages have you written so far?" "Maybe a hundred. How many have you?" He looks crestfallen. "Four." So he prints fewer words to a page, copying them from his favorite book, *Who's a Pest?*, which he has dedicated to me. Generally he writes only title pages: "The Wizard of Oz, by Pip," "Alice in Wonderland, by Pip."

Peggy reads the children my book about a love affair with their grandfather, and they follow the plot with cheerful interest and tolerance. I can't bear to hear it, but they will listen to anything. After enjoying *A Tale of Two Cities*, Steve asked, "How can you stand to have your head chopped off?" Pip explained, "I think Daddy said you kneel."

In the mail is a summons forwarded from the Sheriff of Durham County, scaring me out of my guilty wits (what have I done now to break the law?). It summons me for jury duty, and I reply I am out of town. I do not add that any opinion I might hold would be heretical to God and treasonable to the

State, nor do I admonish the sheriff for his rough language, "Ignore this paper at your peril!" He makes me sound like a criminal being brought to trial instead of an honorable citizen invited to fulfill a duty in service to his county. I respectfully decline.

SEPTEMBER.   In the *TLS*, Philip Larkin refers to a Patagonian proverb that says he who collects enough chamber pots will one day find the Holy Grail.

Philip Larkin says, in his poem "Next, Please":

> Always too eager for the future, we
> Pick up bad habits of expectancy.

A club woman in Raleigh, social leader, president of a literary society, meant to review my latest book for her ladies but made the grave mistake of reading it first. She wrote in shocked reproach. "For shame, Mrs. Bevington! Why are you so *sexy?*"

At first I feared she had sent the letter to the wrong address. Sexy? I talked about love (what else *is* there but a love affair?), marriage, bearing two children, and reading a lot of innocent books. She is too kind; this is compendious praise. But deserved or not, I gladly accept. In the 1960's, I am a sexygenarian.

Self-definition:

"I am so made that I have to believe that everything is simple." —St. Exupéry

"I am the doubter and the doubt." —Emerson

"I am by nature a lover of unfrequented shrines." —Virginia Woolf

"I am a lady who loves decorum." —Madame de Sévigné

"I am slow-witted and lean to the solid and probable." —Montaigne

"I am Sir Oracle,
And when I ope my lips let no dog bark!"   —*Merchant
   of Venice*

OCTOBER.   Montaigne wrote, "I have gone to bed a
thousand times in my own home, imagining that someone
would betray me and slaughter me that very night." My record
is better than Montaigne's. In more than four years alone,
already it adds up to nearly 1500 nights. We have lived in
bad times, Montaigne and I. Yet he sought and found a
"scandalous serenity."

Montaigne lists the advantages of a bad memory (which
he had):

1. One cannot be a good liar.
2. One cannot tell long stories.
3. One forgets offenses.
4. One enjoys places and books a second time round.

And there is a fifth advantage: one forgets the terrors of
the night before.

Today my memory slipped. I quoted Dr. Johnson as saying,
"Sir, a dog's preaching is like a woman walking on her hind
legs. It is not done well; but you are surprised to find it
done at all."
I thought it sounded better that way. It expressed his
towering view.

NOVEMBER.   Harold Nicolson said (in his own
diary) about Pepys: "To my mind Pepys was a mean little
man. Salacious in a grubby way. . . . It is some relief to reflect
that to be a good diarist one must have a little snouty sneaky
mind."

On August 6, 1945, Nicolson wrote with approval: "They have split the atom. They have used it today on a Japanese town." Next day he added, "Viti [his wife]´is thrilled by the atomic bomb. She thinks, and rightly, that it will mean a whole new era." But Viti was furious when Hillary reached the summit of Mt. Everest. She wanted it kept unconquered.

How simply Nicolson proves his case, the cost of being a good diarist, the revelation of how one gives oneself away.

Thorstein Veblen, the phrasemaker. He invented the phrase "trained incapacity," the exact description of some college professors. They have a Ph.D. in it.

Another fine phrase is "the exaltation of the defective." It makes me think of handmade pots and Beat poetry. Handiwork with flaws.

My favorite is "the uneventful diligence of women." Or perhaps "the pecuniarily unfit" (to which I belong). Or, for both sexes of the leisure class, "conspicuous consumption." Each time Veblen was accurate, never admiring.

An appealing kind of writing in France, in a sense notation, is (or was?) *choses vues*. It is, of course, the title of a book by Victor Hugo, from which the name may come: things seen, noted because there they are to look at. In America we haven't much taste for such writing. In prose we require plots and conflicts. In poetry we have little talent for gazing at the view.

Victor Hugo was a passionate observer, partial to death scenes. He had an appetite for extinction, a man sure to be on hand at the sound of a death rattle or the passing of a funeral procession. The *Choses Vues* contains many a moment of mortality, pictured with gusto—the funeral of Napoleon, the death of the Duke of Orléans, the funeral of Mademoiselle Mars, the death of Madame Adélaide, the passing of Balzac. At the final curtain Hugo was unfailing, an absorbed witness and notetaker.

The words which were spoken were simple and grand. The Prince de Joinville said to the king, "Sire, I present to you the body of the Emperor Napoleon." The king replied, "I receive it in the name of France."

I heard a loud and sinister rattling noise. I was in the death chamber of Balzac. . . . The nurse said to me, "He will die at daybreak."

Victor Hugo should have covered his own funeral, one of the grandest and showiest. He lay in state beneath the Arc de Triomphe while all France mourned. Sam Edwards' *Victor Hugo* says two million Frenchmen followed his body to the Pantheon. What a story he could have written of that *chose vue*. Too bad he missed it.

DECEMBER.   Today I read with benefit about the Baroness Burdett-Coutts, an extremely rich Englishwoman and a friend of Dickens, who should have written a Christmas carol with her as the Spirit of Benevolence. Among other benefactions, she took up the cause of the London coster-mongers' donkeys, including yearly prizes for the kind treatment of donkeys in general. She was President of the British Goat Society and did much to encourage British beekeeping. She opened Miss Coutts' Home for Fallen Women. She presided over the Destitute Children's Dinner Society.

When guests were staying in her house, Lady Burdett-Coutts (created a peeress by Victoria) would ask them for the old envelopes they were about to throw into a wastepaper basket. A guest would say, "But they are only old envelopes, Baroness." And Lady Burdett-Coutts would reply, "I know, but I like old envelopes." She cut them up and stuffed pillows with them, which were sent to hospitals to comfort the sick. To use goose feathers would not be kind to the goose.

She was said to be blessed with imperturbability, unmoved (though hers was the great banking name of Coutts & Co.) that she could never learn how to count except on her fingers or how to make out checks. She remained resolutely single till 1881 when, at 67, she married an American forty years younger, who had aided her with the Turkish Compassionate Fund. Since his name was William Ashmead-Bartlett, he dealt with these hyphenations by taking his wife's name. It seems a pity. There is a lovely ring to Mrs. Angela Georgina Burdett-Coutts-Ashmead-Bartlett, besides which she had a sister who married a man named Money and became Mrs. Money-Coutts.

Her marriage was a happy one. She adored William and outlived him, dying at 92, buried with honor in Westminster Abbey for having relieved the distressed.

1969

JANUARY.   Gilbert White kept his Journal for twenty-five years and, simply by making daily entries, set down the data of life.

Mr. White's old servant Thomas came to him one day and said, "Please, sir, I've been and broke a glass."

"Broke a glass, Thomas! How did you do that?"

"I'll show you, sir." He fetched a wine glass which he threw upon the floor, saying, "That's how I broke it, sir."

"Go along, Thomas! You are a great fool. And I was as great a one for asking a foolish question."

Four keys flew off my typewriter, so I took it in to a shop this morning for repair. The manager gave me a quick diagnosis: "The only thing wrong, ma'am, is that you have a screw loose."

P. D. Hagler is a plumber in North Carolina who belongs to one of the motorcycle groups that boom down the highways in black leather jackets, boots, military helmets. His gang is called the Scavengers, and he says he loves being one of hell's angels: "It's the way your hair blows around, the way bugs hit your eyes and teeth." The new Lochinvar rides forth, wind in his hair and bugs in his teeth.

On motorcycles up the road they come:
Small, black, as flies hanging in the heat, the Boys . . .
        —Thom Gunn, "On the Move"

FEBRUARY.   I went to an afternoon movie with Jane and Betty, to see Carson McCullers' "The Heart Is a Lonely Hunter." Jane's husband said, "Who would go to see a picture with a title like that? I know what it says, and I don't want to know."

It devastated me. I do not say so lightly. Alan Arkin as a lonely deaf mute was terrifying. At the end he walked the streets, his face telling the story, his hands at his side spelling out the words for it—the loneliness you die of—then shot himself.

As we left the theater, I was thinking of a cousin of mine, Cousin Georgia, who had been not deaf or mute but desperate. The particular memory had to do with her going to a movie one Saturday afternoon. I never knew her story, more than that Cousin Georgia who was beautiful was unhappy, and she lost her mind as if she had mislaid her purse while watching a picture in a movie house. This occurred after her divorce, after the loss of her child, after she had returned alone to her parents' house. Some plot unfolded on the screen recounting her own tragedy. Raising her fists she stood up in the theater, screamed out "You can't do this to me!" and was frantic, from that moment insane. She lives on in an asylum.

I have a morbid desire to see this film again, learn it by heart. But I don't dare.

To celebrate love on Valentine's Day and the first signs of a Carolina spring, this morning a group of thirty black students at Duke took over the administration building. They barricaded themselves on the first floor, nailing shut the doors. Having brought along gasoline to burn the university records, armed with baseball bats and liquor, they prepared to stay a week in what is called a sit-in. The fear was they would incinerate themselves.

This time Duke stood firm. After a meeting of the faculty, the Provost delivered an ultimatum, and at 6:00 P.M. the Durham police moved into the building, already emptied of the Afro-American students. They had held the place for nine hours. They had made threats and demands, compiled a list of 13 civil rights. They don't want poor grades or any grades at all. They want a Black dormitory, a Black Studies program, a Black adviser, financial assistance, summer coaching. They want to be Black.

Tonight a brawl erupted, a two-hour fight on campus between the police and several thousand students, mostly white, with tear gas, hate, a little bloodshed. This is what college life means—the police and trouble.

Meanwhile the cardinals are singing. The white camellias are in bloom. I stopped my car in the driveway to inspect the green willow almost flattened by a treeful of cedar waxwings.

Most of my students came to classes today, in a temporary lull from riot, so I went on talking. Swich is this world whoso it kan byholde.

M A R C H . A stranger writes: "You help to confirm the theory that life is worth living." I feel guilty at his words, being attracted lately to the opposite theory.

Even my mother's courage, the thing I admired most, strikes me as at least an unprofitable choice. I thought Lizzie's survival a superlative thing (a talent I like in people), proof of endurance, tenacity, something to emulate. But what did she live *for*? No help ever came, no solution. She lived solitary and friendless. I don't know what she proved. Yet, one way or another, I am finding out.

> The saddest thing in life
> Is that the best thing in it should be courage.
> —Frost, "A Masque of Mercy"

A good phrase in a story by Simone de Beauvoir: "The postponement of defeat." She is my age and is thinking it over.

Christopher Columbus, on coming ashore in America, is said to have exclaimed: "During that time I walked among the trees which was the most beautiful thing which I had ever seen."

William Carlos Williams liked Columbus's phrase "beautiful thing" so well he borrowed it 22 times in *Paterson*, Book III. He sounds delirious with saying: "I saw you: Beautiful Thing!," "Beautiful thing and a slow moon," "Beautiful thing, my dove," "Beautiful thing! aflame," "Beautiful thing—that I make a fool of myself—"

> Beautiful Thing!
> Let them explain you and you will be
> the heart of the explanation.

Don't blow your cork, W.C.

APRIL.   Camus said in 1957, when scolded by a journalist: "*Je suis pour la justice, mais, s'il me faut choisir entre la justice et ma mère, je choisis ma mère.*"

I hope I have brought up my sons to take that preferential view. But what is justice?

"My name is Elbow. I do lean upon justice."

A sign outside the entrance to a house on Guess Road: BEWARE OF CATS.

Peggy writes: "Dearest Helen love, I begin to be concerned with pollution. Pollution has been added to a list of devils to be exorcised out of the family day, like tooth decay, ill-temper, and insolence. I am in charge of brushed hair, clean nails, punctuality, the distinction between *like* and *as*, the singularity of *anyone*, information about the body and sexual relations, and the history of the house of Atreus."

MAY.   A North Carolina legislator referred on television to "organized ladies of questionable motive." Pure Southern gallantry. He meant whores.

"Breasts do not constitute the private parts of a woman's body" was the decision of a North Carolina judge. But how private by now is the rest? We have a city ordinance (I think) against bottomless dancing.

Philip my son has just published a book, *Data Reduction and Error Analysis for the Physical Sciences*. It deals with systematic and random errors and uncertainties, exactly as my own books do. The difference is, as a nuclear physicist he is more scientific. I can't understand all his words, but I believe he knows about the errors, even how to eliminate them.

David defines a monograph: "It is a lengthy discourse on an esoteric subject, of interest to few and of value to none. I have written two monographs." He has written two remarkable books on Tudor drama, *From "Mankind" to Marlowe* and *Tudor Drama and Politics*, models of scholarship. Yet he keeps his wit and modesty about him.

My sons seem to me fair, brave, good, talented, modest, loving, accomplished, and extraordinary. Looked at objectively, I mean.

I mind the smell of age that letters get—B.'s letters in the drawer. It doesn't take long, a decade, till they are part of the unreturning past. A letter of David's as an undergraduate at Harvard, January 29, 1952, says, "This is the most amazing day of my life." He had a revelation that day. The light from Damascus hit him at 5:00 P.M. in Harvard Yard, and it revealed, "The meaning of life is that life is really meaningful." I think he got it perfectly right.

JUNE. I've received two letters from Cyril Clemens, editor of the *Mark Twain Journal* in Kirkwood, Missouri, each one announcing, "In recognition of your outstanding contribution to American literature you have been elected A DAUGHTER OF MARK TWAIN. All cordial esteem." The capitals are Mr. Clemens's. The glory is mine, a twice-told daughter. He didn't say what I ought to do about my newly achieved bastardy.

Stephen called Pip a housewife because Pip was sweeping
the doorstep with a broom. Pip hit him hard with the broom
handle, coming down on Steve's knuckles.

I said, "Sticks and stones may break my bones, but words
can never hurt me."

Peggy cried, "No! No! That isn't true."

I said, "Of course it isn't true. I'd take sticks and stones any
time."

David called out from upstairs, "Adult wit. Not for children."

I see that Ogden Nash said it too:

> Sticks and stones may break my bones
> But words can break my heart.

David roams the fields to find wildflowers. Then he recites
their common name and gives them to me. I need to know for
the sake of knowing. I need to know the name of everything,
yet with no talent for recognition. David patiently repeats:
this, my dear, is fleabane. yarrow. healall. tearthumb. St. John's
wort. The oxeye daisy is the ordinary field daisy, think of that.
Samuel Sewall's *Diary* tells how he walked out into his garden
to pick yarrow, either for a love charm or to stop nosebleed.

Pip asked today, "How do you spell sex?" We should have
taken him to the drive-in movie tonight to see "Goodbye,
Columbus" from a Philip Roth novel. On second thought, it
would be easier to spell the word than explain the plot, which
hinged on the use of a diaphragm for lots of naked lovemaking.
E. M. Forster's *A Room with a View* (1908) hinged on a kiss,
one single compromising kiss, regarded as a sacred plighting
of troth. Now both diaphragm and kiss are out of date as
devices. One takes a pill and doesn't worry.

JULY.   They landed on the moon ("We'll get on the
moon first and then find out why"), moonwalkers Neil Arm-
strong and Buzz Aldrin, who came in a poor second, in the

Sea of Tranquillity, too. They bounded among dusty craters planting the American flag, picking up lunar rocks instead of moonbeams, to bring back the moon's story, in case it has one. It looks like a tale told by a lunatic.

They met with no disaster, unlike Ted Kennedy down here on earth, the third Kennedy, the one meant to be our next President. We had the moon and Chappaquiddick, like the title of a lovesong, a dead moon and a dead girl, with closeups of the war dead in Vietnam.

James Dickey covered the moon landing for *Life* and read a poem on television, but he didn't fool me. He never left home.

I saw the devil on the Dick Cavett Show, one named Allen Ginsberg, poet—a most unappetizing, hairy, bearded, gaudy devil. He announced he was paranoid. That was hardly in doubt, the old Howler, the old Beat.

"What's on your mind?" asked Dick Cavett, interviewer.

"Pot."

My choice of lines by Allen Ginsberg is his address to Walt Whitman in "A Supermarket in California":

> I saw you, Walt Whitman, childless, lonely old grubber
> poking among the meats in the refrigerator and
> eyeing the grocery boys. . . .
> I heard you asking questions of each: Who killed
> the pork chops? What price bananas?

In *The Anatomy of Melancholy*, Robert Burton lists as causes of melancholy, in this order: God, bad angels and devils, witches and magicians, stars, old age, parents, and bad diet.

The real cause is missing. Solitude is the thing itself.

The consolations of philosophy:

Erasmus: "To live at all is a kind of rashness, but it is better to live than not to live."

Loren Eiseley, *The Unexpected Universe:* "Each one of us is a statistical impossibility around which hovers a million other lives that were never destined to be born."

Chaucer, *Monk's Tale:*

"Allas," quod he, "allas, that I was wrought!"
Therwith the teeris fillen from his yen.

Montaigne: "We leave this world as we came into it, crying." But that is hardly fair. Newborn babies haven't learned to laugh.

SHELLEY AND THE NEWBORN BABY

Shelley at Oxford, his head full of Plato,
Stopped a woman on Magdalen Bridge.
"Will your baby tell us of pre-existence,
Madam?"—at which this newborn sage,
This mulish infant, refused to answer.
"How provoking!" said Shelley, "at its age."

But suppose the child had actually spoken.
"There isn't any," it might have said,
Refuting Plato, confounding Wordsworth,
Poets alive and philosophers dead.
Shelley would have stared, indignant.
"How provoking!" Shelley would have said.

AUGUST.   H. L. Mencken visited the battlefield of Armageddon. The vast barrier of the Syrian mountains ends there in the promontory of Mount Carmel. Below the narrow pass, the land of Palestine widens into a flat plain where all the battles occurred. Here the Hittites met the Egyptians; the Egyptians met the Persians; the Persians met the Greeks; and

the Jews were slaughtered by everybody. In 610 B.C., Josiah,
King of Judah, perished on the bloody field of Armageddon. Its
latest battle was as recent as 1918 when Allenby and the Turks
fought all over it.

"There is probably no more likely battlefield on earth,"
Mencken wrote. But he found no markers or flags, no monuments, no souvenirs (nothing like Gettysburg). The soil he
thought was the color of blood.

So, on the last day, "the great day of God," the Judgment
Day, the last battle will be fought at Armageddon between
the powers of good and evil—the struggle with God that Satan
is scheduled to lose. It sounds like a proper, well-tried battlefield for the battle of the End of Time. Till then, evil will go
on winning as usual, evil and the forces of destruction.

I spent an hour with Bertrand Russell tonight, watching him
on educational television. What an odd way to visit an old
friend, whom I haven't seen since the happy day B. and I
spent with him in Richmond in 1952. Now B. is dead. And this
is my last meeting on earth with Bertrand Russell, sure to be.
Neither of us will get to heaven, either.

Naturally he looks older at 97, tired and frail as he was not
seventeen years ago in London. The bark of a laugh is gone.
The familiar pipe is missing. Since the first time he visited my
house in Durham, when he was 79, he has published twenty-
two books. He has endured, without many sustaining beliefs
except in himself, without faith in God, without hope for
peace. To have faith, Russell once told me, is to believe without evidence. He rejected it. Nothing bored him more than a
Christian. I remember the conviction in his voice.

On television he appeared at his latest home in Wales. There
were shots of Pembroke Lodge in Richmond Park, where we
three walked together back to his childhood. Leonard Woolf
(who died the other day) and other old guys spoke to praise
him: "He takes his dignity for granted." Russell's mind is
sharp, clear, the quickest mind I've ever known, still unim-
paired. It is good to have a skinny little sandpiper body and
brains to spare. His eyesight and hearing seem keen. He lives.

He said he would speak in this broadcast as a human being.

That was consoling. He began by reading the words, "Since Adam ate the apple, man has never refrained from any folly of which he was capable." Not so consoling.

The human race will not survive, he said, unless man finds a solution by the end of the century. "Is all this to end in trivial horror?" Russell will die in the futile attempt to save us.

"Remember your humanity and forget the rest," he said. Endearing to listen to. But he is old, as if ready not to take the next breath. Would he kiss me now? Sure he would.

Bertrand Russell was writing these words for me (at least I take them to myself) in the month and year of my birth: "What is absolutely vital to me is the self-respect I get from work—when (as often) I have done something for which I feel remorse, work restores me to a belief that it is better I should exist than not exist."

His *Autobiography* shows the incredible vitality of the man. I marvel at the passion of his dedicatory verse "To Edith" written in his own hand, announcing he has found ecstasy at last. "I have found both ecstasy and peace. . . . I know what life and love may be." Ecstasy, at 94?

SEPTEMBER.   I walked behind a titillating girl on East Campus. She wore tight patched jeans, pullover sweater, long Alice-in-Wonderland curls to her shoulders, hips swinging freely as she strode to the library. We reached the door together, and she turned to reveal a face covered with a full beard. Without the face, who could tell? Only if she had worn a miniskirt.

W. S. Gilbert defined a man as a monkey shaved. It wasn't true in his bearded time—or of Gilbert himself, who wore a mustache and sideburns—and it is grossly untrue now. No monkey would submit to all that hair on his face, even to look like Tolstoi. (We've come a long way, monkey.)

———

Somebody telephoned at 10:30 last night, a man's low menacing voice. He said, "If you are still in your house at midnight, lady, look out. We're coming to get you."

I didn't call the sheriff, more annoyed at being threatened than actually afraid. At midnight I was still here, wakeful but unarmed. The Pattons had a telephone call a few nights ago with the promise to blow up their house. They called the police, as Lewis tells me I must always do. But he doesn't live in my countryside, with the pioneer life and no protection from the Indians.

I wonder if I would have loaded and used my gun. I'm a slow draw.

The plumber, Mr. Mincey, came to fix the toilet. As he was leaving, he stopped at the door. "How long have you lived here alone, ma'am?"

"Five years and more."

"Yesterday," said Mr. Mincey, "I was fixing a lady's toilet and I asked her how long she'd been a widow. 'Six months,' she said and started to cry. I put my arm around her and she laid her head on my shoulder and cried for five minutes. Now, Mrs. Bevington," he said, "if you want a shoulder to cry on, ma'am, why here I am."

"Do you charge extra for this service?"

"No, ma'am. No charge."

At that I laughed. I couldn't help it. I said, "Thank you very much, Mr. Mincey. What I really need is a shoulder to laugh on."

So we had an hour and a half with England's Royal Family, brought to us by Sears, Roebuck, whose slogan is: "You've changed lately. So has Sears." Sears has gone royal. Royalty has gone common. I too have changed for the worse: we were in it together.

The sights were 9000 guests at Buckingham Palace, the Queen on the royal train, the royal yacht, at the opera, interrupted from time to time by pictures from Sears' bath and slumber shop. I saw Balmoral, where one forgets "the world and its sad turmoils," according to Queen Victoria. The Royal Family had an outdoor picnic—hamburgers.

Elizabeth said "like they do," but television may require this grammatical usage. She seemed a pleasant matron and no actress, given to remarking at intervals "Thank you very much." Prince Philip came through wooden, Prince of Wales solid, Anne sullen, little princes mere props. They needed a better script. So did Sears.

God save royalty. The justification for saving it was spelled out: though the power of the sovereign no longer matters, the power of her office excludes a dictator in England or a usurper. Whatever happened to divine right? And why have we no Elizabethan Age, no Elizabethan poetry? We had the Edwardians. We had the Georgians, honoring George V. Elizabeth II, where are your poets?

O C T O B E R .   Once again I'm teaching a course in Creative Writing (you mean how to *write?*), with ten students meeting in my office twice a week before lunch. I figure that hunger will keep them from staying all afternoon, though we drink tea during class and sometimes eat doughnuts.

On opening day, I was frightened. As Brendan Behan said of a bad moment of his own, "Not all the sins of my past life passed in front of me, but as many as could get room in the queue." After years of trying, I still don't know how to teach. I lack patience, decorum, and the sense to hold my tongue. "Keep quiet, listen, even if you choke," I tell myself, but today when I shut my mouth there was nothing to hear. They sat silent around the table, eight men and two girls, waiting for me to talk. That is what I'm paid for, to teach, to say something (preferably omniscient).

So I said we would start by agreeing to omit rudeness, scurrility, spite, railing, scorn, anger, malice, revenge, gracelessness, and general bad manners in our dealings with each other. We were not here to defend the pass at Thermopylae. We were here to laugh and enjoy. Our laughter would be benevolent. Anyone misjudging the occasion would be ejected from the room, myself included. Creative writing was a fraud otherwise. Some call it a fraud anyway, but it seems to me that people are creative.

"We might follow Shaw's advice," I said: " 'In the right key one can say anything; in the wrong key, nothing.' " Nobody tumbled to the joke. Did Shaw, scorner of mankind, ever intentionally soften his voice or mind his manners?

Above all, I said, we were to feel free to speak out, safe among friends. The hard thing is to give criticism. The hardest thing is to take it—to be exposed as a poor storyteller, as an inarticulate and unintelligible poet, to be guilty of confused plots and mixed metaphors. Shortcomings are therefore permitted.

I tell them to make a poem visible. The thing must be seen. Then Ned makes his mother visible or psychedelic in "Oedipus and Mom," written in anger—"Mama, you choose my women." Scott attacks his date for having lips like a red Victorian pincushion (visible enough). He wants to rape the hymen of her mind and deposit an idea there. Charlie either advises or objects to castrating God, it's doubtful which. Andy uses *pervert* when he means *perverse*, making marvelous nonsense.

I quote Coleridge: "When a man is unhappy, he writes damned bad poetry, I find." And Harvey writes about black people walking under black umbrellas in the white rain.

One poet in the class is like Jules Renard's sparrow: "A delightful little bird that does not sing. When it has said 'Peep!' it thinks it has said everything there is to say."

They write two kinds of short stories. They write of childhood (grandparents, school recess, a pal in the third grade, first love). And they write of now (a wild party, smoking grass, a sexual encounter, Vietnam, painful weekend at Princeton, disillusionment with rioting at Duke last spring—"I never knew what we were fighting about"—of anger, hopes coming apart).

The two kinds of narrative differ in language and tone. The past is shown as poignant, simple, happy. The present is harsh, stark, drunken, messy in relationships. Today's tale, unwinding presto, presto, presto, ends unhappy ever after.

I wonder: is this what the child grows up to?

Having written a poem—that is, words arranged on the page that don't look at least like prose—they say, "What is this?" They want it identified. Without pattern, shape, form, rhyme, structure, or content, who can tell what manner of thing it is?

My students compose what I call "bed poems," but I'm sorry they are so disconsolate in tone, the experience so bleak. They write about a prostitute with a "yellowed bra" who farts; about girls with swelling breasts "wet-nippled like the moon" who are unfaithful. No fun at all. I remind them of Donne's delight in his mistresses, of Herrick's gratitude to his Julias. The students would find it sentimental to enjoy being in love, romantics that they are. They say, "We look with shallow eyes of unlove." After class I hunt up Keats to see how old he was when he wrote those three sonnets "On Woman" ("God! she is like a milk-white lamb that bleats / For man's protection"). He wasn't yet twenty. What a relief.

Robert Graves, dealing in statistics, declares that no more than one person in twenty is capable of knowing what a poem is about. We are eleven in the class, counting teacher. More than one in twenty write poems; everybody writes poems, though whether one in twenty knows what he is writing about is not always clear. I like these comfortless facts—Henry Adams, too, saying you can't teach more than one person in ten, since the rest aren't teachable. I never question the accuracy of the man who arrives at such exact computations.

Anyway, my students' poems don't have to be read to be understood. They have to be decoded.

Wallace Stevens: "The plum survives its poems."

NOVEMBER.   My student Arthur has written a moon-poem full of spaceflight. It makes Andy and Ned mad, because they deplore the space program that uses money needed on earth for relieving poverty. The moon be damned, they say. A man dares to walk on another planet and they, aged twenty, eager to be poets, scowl in fury and turn their backs, outraged. (Jules Renard: "Put a little moon into what you write.")

A man in orbit can see the moon in one window, the sun in another, the earth in a third. He must feel like God. Not Andy and Ned; they feel sick. We're having trouble getting moonlight and poets together these days.

Harvey looks like an African warrior with bushy hair and a necklace of elephant teeth. He is amiable, friendly, smiling, though his poems dwell on the plight of being black. "To be black is to be misunderstood" is the theme of one poem (which may or may not have been inspired by Emerson's "Self-Reliance": "To be great is to be misunderstood"). Harvey's poem goes on for thirteen pages, restating the phrase in various groupings down the page. He expects words to sound better the oftener they're repeated. "Harvey," I say, "to be white is to be misunderstood. To be female—I could write thirteen pages on that. To be Jewish, Chinese, to be a human being is to be misunderstood." He laughs, as he always laughs. "This is my hangup."

The class agrees about hangups, to which everybody is entitled. They don't like him to take the Black party line. Harvey enjoys being the center of our concern. I call them his black-and-white poems.

Bill has a block about writing but takes the course anyway, and I let him. Writers needn't write in my course. I read his outpourings all last year: now when it's appropriate to write he says he can't. He brings me white narcissus instead. And a note to say:

> now that I understand
> you a little—I don't
> understand me at all.

Taylor is the one whose grandmother weighs three hundred pounds. In a story of his, she took the Christmas dinner fresh from the hot oven, including, he said, the cranberry sauce, crisp celery, and iced tea. She then gave him a three-hundred-pound hug and enveloped him "in several inches of bosom and lilac toilet water." "Must have drowned hell out of him," said Andy.

Taylor has dark eyes, a fondness for pink shirts, and a love for Linda (not in the class). His habit of putting his head down on the table makes me ask, "Taylor, are you laughing or weeping?" "Laughing," he says, raising a convulsed face. His story of a student exposing himself to a girl in the Duke library produced not laughter but astonishment. "Where?" we asked. "Beside the Xerox machine," said Taylor, and at that everyone roared and Taylor blushed.

"I don't believe a word of it," I said, "not of anybody named John Jacob Bellringer."

"Neither do I," said Taylor.

About to marry soon, he plans to hold the wedding ceremony in Westminster Abbey or, better still, at Little Gidding.

Bobby's real name is Rose, a Jewish girl sensitive to slights but with a good armor. She is bright, ambitious to become a Ph.D. ("even if I marry"), aware she will not waste many tears over creative writing. Her best story so far, about being jilted, saddens her because it is an unhappy, true experience. "You say young writers too often sound bitter and miserable," she tells me. "I honestly wanted to write about happiness."

Arthur is a gentleman from Virginia. It worries him that, turned twenty-one, he has not yet been hopelessly in love, not all passion spent but still to spend. This predicament he fears limits his poetry in intensity. "I sing the song of in-experience," he writes, tongue in cheek, not very rueful about it. "I am young enough / To wear my trousers rolled." That's the kind of Prufrock I like.

Margo sits at my right hand, blackhaired and beautiful, dispensing tea. She too writes about love, in declarative sentences: "I remember the first time he kissed me." The radiant difference between her and the others is that being in love makes her happy, serene. To her it belongs with the true and the absolute. Nobody doubts her word. She merely seems to the class well-adjusted and implausible. ("I thought," said my Uncle Toby, "that love had been a joyous thing.")

After a fashion, as a way of putting it, I finished my book this afternoon [*The House Was Quiet and the World Was Calm*], weeping my way to the end. I used to smoke cigarettes at the typewriter and drink iced tea. Now my tears make me cry (Jules Renard asks about tears, "What happens to all the tears we do not shed?"), a whole puddle, always ready, even when the memories are comic. To say with Eliot the time is always now is to lie. The time for me is *then*. *Now* is merely a question of what to set down about the past on a blank piece of paper.

The house was quiet and the world was calm, Wallace Stevens said, *because it had to be*. The title is ironic but will be misread, misunderstood. What quiet house? What calm world?

Years ago when B. teased me with the prediction it would take 600 pages to finish what I had started—an appalling idea, since by then I'd barely observed my life up to the age of eight—he was right. It took 600 pages, three books, for the whole divine comedy of the absurd.

Having searched the manuscript to root out adverbs (terribly passionately frantically) and my habitual outcry at every crisis, "Oh, my God," "Dear merciful God," "God Almighty!"— a vocabulary of peace and calm but repetitious—at least I've found what the theme is: survival. Though I never planned it, proceeding by guess and by God, each book ends on a question of survival, the attempt to stay alive (and to seek love) in a destructive world like mine.

The last three words of the last book tell of my son Philip's survival after a near-fatal car accident, the only words in my world that can matter: "He will live."

Once in a moon a solution comes—a solution day ("Well shone, Moon"). And my woes then lull, then leave off. Oliver, my chairman, wrote, after predicting this would never happen: "The Personnel Committee of the English Department has recommended that you be promoted to the rank of professor effective in the session 1970–71." Say that with sixteen marbles in your mouth.

As we cordially agree, I fit into none of Duke's strict categories: I'm not a man, not a Ph.D., not a scholar. Women professors are an odd and rare few; the specifications are meant to fit a white Protestant Anglo-Saxon male about forty. It's a strange victory, though "full" professor sounds giddy enough. What about the compleat professor? William Jay Smith says,

> And a delicate wind is blowing, forever blowing
> In and out of the trees and through the Professor's head.

The wind that blows is a fickle wind, warming at times and southerly.

DECEMBER.   My boy Harvey wrote this poem about me. The class criticized it closely, approving, calling it honest, truthful, fair, Harvey's best writing to date—*except* for the word *führer*. They hated that. "Take it out!" they said. I said, "Oh, he only means a dictator." "Take it out!" they said. "It's offensive." Harvey laughed. He loves being criticized and never changes a word.

A bit of class

> Head-of-the-table teacher,
> Her left-hand emphases with demi-doughnuts done,
> (and sipping tea)
> EXPLICATES
> line   by   line,
> trying to discover what words will do.
>
>> Images, symbols, similes, metaphors—
>> conflicting and inconsistent.
>
>> No! no! NO!

Yeats would not have it!
Clarity, clarity, clarity
she expounds and pounds.

Falseface führer,
pitiless yet pitying,
praising within.

But *good* poetry is so, so difficult to write.
And she knows
yet she cannot, must not, will not
countenance less-than-perfection.

Mask slipping, she sighs,
"After this, let's have doughnuts and love."

At least he didn't call me a witch.